Conspiracy to Riot

Conspiracy to Riot

The Life and Times of One of the Chicago 7

Lee Weiner

Belt Publishing

Printed in the United States of America
First Edition

ISBN: 978-1-948742-68-9

Belt Publishing
3143 W. 33rd Street #6
Cleveland, Ohio 44109
www.beltpublishing.com

Cover art by David Wilson
Book design by Meredith Pangrace

Contents

Introduction

Depending on when you start counting from, it's been more than fifty years since I joined with others of my generation in the work of repairing the world. Most of those years were spent trying to make things better for people who were being hurt by the cruelties of economic, racial, and sexual oppression; by a brutal and unnecessary war; and by a politics beholden to wealth that ignored or actively plotted against social justice. Two of those years—1968 and 1969—propelled me, along with seven other men, to the forefront of America's culture wars and changed my life forever.

Because of my experiences in the 1960s, I have an admittedly odd relationship to politics these days. Back then everyone was brave. We were all certain that we were building a better, freer, more equitable America. "Social justice" wasn't an abstract principle in some political philosophy course; it was something to fight for in the streets. There was a war that had to be stopped. And for some of us, including me, long hair, beads, arrests, and jail time were all proofs of our political commitment. We frightened our parents terribly.

Today I engage in politics like some demented, obsessed observer. I'm forever watching, worrying, calculating, and analyzing, but I'm kept away from most direct political work by a barrier made up of memories of what was and what might have been. My impulses to act politically are usually (but thank the goddess, not always) thwarted by the enduring cynicism and wariness of a political refugee who now lives in a familiar but strange land.

After unexpectedly surviving a modest, but still real enough, civil war, I have never been able to completely reconcile my leftover feelings, my long-held values, and my ideals with my everyday life in America. I often feel oddly displaced. (And all those radio stations playing hits from the sixties and seventies, and the aging rockers who are still touring, don't help.) Despite my best efforts to stay connected to what is really happening, I am easily caught unawares coming out of an engaging evening movie, startled to remember where I am and who I am now. The past—its noise, energy, hope, anger, and risk—is always lurking in my head, often more present than whatever it is I'm supposed to be seeing and doing and feeling in the here and now.

But I'm not a fool. I understand that in many other places, at other times, and even now, I would at best still be imprisoned for my confrontations with state power. Those confrontations started small: shouting through a megaphone about freedom of speech to a crowd on a college campus; joining picket lines in support of the sit-ins against segregation in southern cities. But they grew into years of organizing work—which included demonstrations and arrests—with people in poor communities to help them fight back against the local government's deliberate lies, denigration, and neglect. Those confrontations grew into much larger demonstrations against an unjust war and the abuse of power by the state and the rich, demonstrations that demanded changes to a demeaning, ugly, oppressive culture. That led to violence in the streets, more arrests, and eventually to a famous, raucous political trial involving some my friends, where the federal government's failure to silence or jail us for very long still shows that people do in fact have the capacity and the responsibility to speak out and fight back against cruel and unjust power. My life since those faraway days has instead been fairly successful. I've integrated with the real world well enough to have mostly earned my living by doing work for politicians and nonprofit organizations that I can defend to myself as "acceptable."

Most of the people I knew back then might not agree with my notions of politically "acceptable" work. So many of us were certain that we knew the definitions and boundaries of what good, or important, or useful work were, the exact ways one had to see and talk about the world in order to move the revolution, or at least positive political change, forward. And, as it seems for a lot of people now, we weren't shy about making serious moral judgments about the things our friends might be doing or saying that didn't match our expectations.

Still, even the best work I did for many years could only be described as "ameliorative"—simply trying to make things a little better for some people in some places in an immediate way. My oldest son once marveled that I somehow had been able to mostly make a living and lead a life that continued to revolve around my self-chosen identity as "political." He wondered aloud how I had managed it, but at the time I didn't have much of an acceptable sounding answer for him. First, I didn't really think I had managed to have anything close to the sort of politically charged and directed life that he thought I had lived. If I compared my life to how many other people lived, though, I was more often engaged in politics. I had been driven, tortured, gladdened, and brought to joy or rage by politics. I'd sometimes made fateful decisions about how I would lead my life based on whatever my understanding of politics and possibility were in a particular moment. But I was also held back from giving as honest an answer as my son deserved because I was—and am still now—vulnerable to the guilt and loss that was all too often involved in it all. And in Chicago in the late sixties, my son was one of the victims of my breaking so many promises I'd made or implied—most specifically to his mother and to him—before I was willingly swept away into a different life.

So I sort of gave him half an answer involving luck. Because of course in those days, if you were going to survive a dissident political life, and then be able to make up for at least part of the hurt your earlier choices had caused to the people you loved, you had to be lucky.

It also helped that the times and stars have been well-aligned for me. I didn't end up dead, and I didn't end up in a prison cell for too long. The world was rich and forgetful enough to make it possible for me to just slip back into it. Though I'm not oblivious to the fact that over the years, I was able to escape the most terrible consequences of my work against state power in part because I'm a white, heterosexual, cisgender man with all sorts of privileges and educational credentials, raised in relative comfort, and who has mostly been able to live and work in social contexts where my Jewish identity wasn't an obvious handicap. So I was basically able to walk away from direct political work when I wanted to. Nobody much noticed or cared. And I simply continued on with my day-to-day life.

Despite my quiet existence now, I remain committed to political change in America. I still become as enraged, nauseous, hopeful, and desperate at political and economic news as ever. But now I live my political life in the shadows. This book is an attempt to walk out from those shadows and speak to others about times and experiences that I believe have some direct relevance to more current political dreams and the attempts to make them real. It's written especially to try to help strengthen people who want to or are already actively resisting some of today's ugly political assaults and demands.

Because here's the thing: what happened on the streets of Chicago in August 1968 when people rose up to act together against war and injustice, and what happened in the trial that followed to blame and punish whomever the government decided could and should be blamed, was far from a one-time thing. The trial captivated the nation at the time precisely because many citizens understood—and rejected—what the government was trying to do. We emerged from the trial largely unscathed. But the government's fight against freedom of speech and the people who want something different, something more, something better, has continued. Of course, state authorities are still using their power to oppress dissent, to lie, to create "alternative facts," and to try to define away the legitimacy and importance of political and moral criticism from anyone who shouts such unwelcome truths.

It doesn't change. Government and economic power will work to sustain, legitimate, and enlarge their control. They will try to destroy, humiliate, denigrate, or delegitimize any alternative solutions dissenters might offer that threaten existing power. But people have resisted power in the not-so-distant past. Some of what we did worked, and some of it didn't. Some of it might make sense now, and some of what we did might only highlight paths that didn't work for us and aren't likely to work any better now. But I believe it's worth spending a little time remembering some of those past struggles and figuring out what lessons might be relevant to today's politics.

Chapter 1

A Semi-Tough Jewish Kid
from Chicago's South Side

I was born in 1939 in a neighborhood on Chicago's South Side that was neither the best nor the worst part of the city. My family lived on Seventy-Fourth and Colfax on the top floor of a three-story six-flat attached to another one just like it. Our block was just barely on the right side of the tracks and in back of what seemed to me then to be a large coal yard. The Illinois Central, the "IC," ran up Exchange Avenue to the Loop just on the other side. We were only four slightly rundown city blocks west of Lake Michigan and Rainbow Beach, with its piled together collection of big rocks and cement blocks that formed a little jetty out into the water. You could jump off those rocks into the lake, and in the summers I often did.

Our street was full of three-story apartment buildings like ours, mostly filled with young families and their children—all of us kids who were the unknowing froth on the front edge of the coming baby boomer wave. It wasn't the greatest or fanciest place to live, but there were unexpected pleasures. My third-floor bedroom window faced east, and I spent many summer nights watching the thunderstorms and rain and lightning rush from the nearby lake toward the city and my bedroom. If I looked south, I could watch the flames coming from the steel mills' tall chimneys compete with the lightning in the sky. It was a private joy, those stunning flashes of light across the thick clouds and darkness as I waited and hoped for the next one and the one after that.

Practically everybody in our immediate area was Jewish— or at least it seemed that way on our side of the street. At

Christmas, there were glittering trees in many windows of the double-wide apartment building right across the street. My younger sister Rayna and I could look out at them forever. In Chicago, that was about as much cultural diversity as you were going to get and still be sure you were safe.

My family's immigrant story was similar to most of my neighbors', and it informed the politics that would dominate my later life. My maternal great-grandfather, Abraham Moshe Tasemkin, left Russia in 1890 or 1891 for America, and then more or less disappeared somewhere in the new country. By 1893 his wife, my great-grandmother Esther, who had my then three- or four-year-old grandfather with her, walked away from their village *shtetl* to find him. The family story is that she tracked her husband down to the South Side of Chicago where he was living with another woman, and she threw that woman out a second-story window.

All the stories I heard about my maternal great-grandparents praised their stubborn strength and perseverance. They had five more children—all daughters—but never slowed down. Like many immigrants, Abraham and Esther started their own business. It was a furniture store that catered to a growing, ethnically mixed, working-class neighborhood—Irish, Italians, Scandinavians, Poles, and Jews—around the Calumet River and the newly built steel mills where many people in the community worked.

Most of my great-grandfather's daughters worked in his furniture store, along with their husbands and some of their children. When I was a young kid walking the streets in South Chicago with my mother, father, and sister, shopping or visiting my great-grandfather's store, Jewish shopkeepers would come out of their stores and tell me how much I looked like him and my grandfather. They were right: when I was maybe twelve or thirteen, my sister Rayna found an old photo of my grandfather wearing a bowler hat and one of those too-tight suit jackets you always see in sepia-toned photos from long ago. She asked our mother why I was dressed up in such funny clothes.

My grandfather, the child my great-grandmother carried with her out of Russia, was Nathan Barney Tasemkin, and he left home at sixteen to work. He ultimately established his own furniture store on Forty-Sixth and Ashland in the "Back of the Yards" neighborhood, which was then filled with Irish, Poles, Ukrainians, Lithuanians, and other middle Europeans who worked in the stockyards. The whole area was soaked in that particular smell of animals and slaughter that sometimes wafted south and east toward my own South Shore neighborhood, but the Back of the Yards was an altogether different South Side neighborhood from mine. Jews might own some of the stores in the area, but they didn't live there. The street boundaries between different white ethnic groups, each with their own national-based churches, were more rigid. The Back of the Yards was more uniformly working-class, filled with stockyard and factory workers, policemen, and other people who worked for the city in one job or another.

My grandparents had three daughters. The oldest, my aunt Bea, was short, heavy, and plain looking. She did the books in the back office of my grandfather's growing furniture business instead of going to college. The youngest, my aunt Sadelle, was a little taller and thinner than her sisters. Ferociously smart, she went to the University of Chicago, becoming interested enough in the sciences that she did some junior work on what eventually became the Manhattan Project. My mother Ruth was the middle daughter—short, pretty, and smart. She married before her older sister, which upset her father. She also graduated from the University of Chicago. She loved books and politics and her family and friends. She cooked under duress, hated housework, and fled the house to work as a substitute teacher on the same day my sister started kindergarten.

My father, Herman, was also Jewish and from Chicago, but his childhood was very different from my mother's. The child of an Ashkenazi father and a Sephardic mother, he was raised in an Orthodox home in one of the Jewish parts of the West Side. He spoke Yiddish and some Ladino, but the language I heard from him most often was West Side Chicago Streetwise.

My father dropped out of Northwestern University to take over his father's commercial painting business after his father died of lead poisoning (paint was all lead-based then). He quickly encountered problems that a striving college boy might not have anticipated. The Painters' Union in Chicago had been mobbed up very early on, and he was dependent on that union for his workers. If he really wanted to run a successful business, he needed to become a "friend" of the organized crime guys who controlled the union, not just someone who hired painters. He had to establish friendships and often pay the people who dominated not only that union, but also the decisions about who got contracts to paint in the big buildings downtown. Some of those new friends were people he remembered from his old neighborhood; others were Italian. Whatever he didn't already know from growing up on Chicago's tough West Side, he quickly learned as he managed to make a living as a commercial and residential interior decorating contractor.

A regular part of my childhood involved hearing my father talk and tell stories about money and power and different ways of being Jewish. He would tell me about hard drinking with Sicilians, about Jewish mobsters like the Purple Gang in Detroit or the Murder Incorporated tough guys out of Brownsville, and about how Sam Bronfman's decision during Prohibition to ship his whiskey in small boats across Lake Erie from Canada to Meyer Lansky's waiting trucks helped turn Scotch whisky into an everyday American drink. I heard about the Painters' Union and the Outfit, which is what the Italian organized crime syndicate in Chicago was called. He shared what he knew about the details, rewards, and risks in running money for the mob—cleaning their cash from gambling, dope, and wherever else so it could more easily and safely be used for buying things like legitimate businesses and commercial real estate when using cash might make sellers a little uncomfortable. But of course the cash was always there for payoffs to cops and judges and politicians, and that reality was often used to explain his perspective on how Chicago's politics really worked.

From my father I learned the family backgrounds of lots of prominent Jews in Chicago. I learned about a longtime liberal Congressman named Sid Yates, whose father-in-law's pickle trucks were used to carry liquor during Prohibition. Then there was Marshall Korshak, an elected state senator who my father assumed spent at least some time protecting his Outfit-connected brother Sidney's interests from the possible interference of state regulatory authorities and the police. There was also Jake Arvey, a tremendously powerful leader of the city's Democratic Party, whose union friends helped make sure the "right" voters voted, electing only people who went along with how things were already working. I also heard some choice tales about Henry Crown and his son Lester, billionaire industrialists from a family that had started out selling gravel and sand to builders for making concrete. The Crowns also had to have their own special union friends.

Connections, my father taught me, were everything in Chicago. Without union or Outfit friends (many were often both) success in retail politics or in businesses involving trucks and unskilled labor was impossible. Having guys available who were tough enough to make sure people voted the right way, or who could walk serious picket lines and stop anybody trying to cross were the least of it. The wrong person wanting to run for office could be warned or threatened. Trucks could burn. There was still a tangible connection between Jewish and Italian mobsters in Chicago in the fifties, but those street level connections had already been withering—the Jews were increasingly only involved in the near "white-collar" work of casino gambling, running money, and corrupt politics. My father would sometimes tell me he wanted to spit whenever he heard Lansky's name because he believed Lansky had sided with the New York Sicilians and the Chicago mob boss Tony Accardo against the Jews in the Purple Gang and those in Chicago and Brooklyn.

I would later figure out, with the help of a therapist or two, that my father was not what anybody might reasonably consider a terrific dad. But he sure gave me some solid lessons about life as it is, rather than how you might like it to be. A lot of fathers teach their kids how to drive, but my father could easily put the fix in to make sure I passed my driving exam because he was on a first-name basis with the guy giving the road test at the city's motor vehicle department in the neighborhood. That guy had once been part of a union crew that had worked for my dad, and he also ran poker games for some Outfit guys on weekends at the VFW. After I passed, my father told me to fold a five-dollar bill around my license if a traffic cop stopped me. He also taught me the differences between the bribes one offered to the "park police" (who patrolled the Outer Drive and the series of connected parks and boulevards that were independently controlled by the Chicago Park District on the North and South Sides) and the regular Chicago city police.

I never found a way to ask my father the right questions, so I never learned the details about his relationship to organized crime. But the ties were obviously there. In 1950, when I was eleven years old, my father decided to leave his work as a painting contractor and run a bar on the West Side with Al

Coletta, one of his old painting union crew chiefs. Al was a tough guy, and his position as a union crew chief was mostly a job he'd been given as a semi-retirement gift for all of his earlier, harder, more brutal work for the Outfit. On my occasional visits to the bar, I remember being shown a large back room that had tables pushed together in the middle and high stacks of liquor boxes along the walls. My father explained that friends of his and Al's sometimes used the place to count and bundle betting slips they had collected from around the neighborhood.

But owning the bar didn't last. The mob guys apparently decided that the back room of the bar, with its direct access to the alley, would work well for bringing in "dope"—which then only meant heroin—so it could be packaged up for distribution. When the mob informed Al and my father of their plans, they balked. Betting slips were one thing, but my father and Al wouldn't agree to let the place be used for dope. A couple of days after that, two young men with sawed-off shotguns came in to rob the place. From behind the bar, my father asked them if they really knew where they were, because the way the back room was sometimes used made the bar sort of a "protected space." One of them said they knew exactly where they were, and he walked over with his shotgun. My father told Al, who was at the other end of the bar where the cash register was, to give them the money. The guy swung his weapon toward Al, who nodded to my father, then reached into the cash drawer, pulled out a .32 snub-nosed revolver, and shot the robber in the face. My father had dived to the floor so he wasn't exactly sure what happened next. The other robber fired his shotgun. Then Al got around to the front of the bar, shot the first robber again, and then chased the second one down the street. By the time my father got out of the bar, Al had apparently shot the one he was chasing in the back, flipped him over with his foot, and shot him again in the face. My father went over to Al, told him that he had just bought my father's half of the bar, and then called my grandfather to get a job at the furniture store. He was a furniture salesman for the rest of his working life, and I learned one of the really important differences between being "connected" and being "friends" with the Outfit—friends could walk away.

Around this same time, my parents decided Rayna and I were too old to continue sharing the second bedroom in the apartment, and I was moved into my own bedroom in the quickly refurbished enclosed back porch. The porch was connected to the rest of the apartment by a flimsy glass-paned door and a couple of windows to our dining room. Every month or so, my mother and father's cousins and friends used to play cards in there around the big table. And through the half-closed windows between the dining room and the porch, I lay awake on my bed and learned a lot more about what the world was like and what it might mean to be a grown-up.

When my father and his friends dominated the card table, I learned about the aggravations of laying off bets on weekends. I also learned about the rise of certain neighborhood lawyers who were now working more closely with people tied to the mob, people you might talk to if you wanted to buy some expensive thing a little cheaper than you could find in a store, or if you needed help taking care of some inconsequential thing with the city. All of the stories were about everyday things in their worlds, nothing unusual, and all of it represented completely reasonable ways of being a Jew and making a living in the world—of getting by.

When my mother's old friends played cards, I learned about very different ways of being Jewish. A whole group of my mother's friends seemed to be old Communist Party members, and some of them had even been street and union organizers. Everybody knew Studs Terkel; they had all raised money for Paul Douglas in his runs for the Senate, and lots of the women worked for the city's welfare department. Nobody taught in the schools. Nobody worked in the unions anymore. All that had ended for them during the Red Scare of the late forties and early fifties. When those friends were playing cards, I would listen to their jokes and stories about politics, Zionism, Marx, Lenin, Trotsky, and this union guy or that union guy. They would often use different degrees of derogatory English and Yiddish terms toward the kinds of jobs they now did for a living, referring back to when someone had left the "other work" (an oblique reference to whatever they might have done for the Party). I remember hearing from my mother's friend Eddie Goldberg about how it was better to speak to a crowd from the top of a car because you could help focus the crowd, see when the cops moved in, and then run off in any direction. Years later that turned out to be helpful advice.

Many of my parents' friends were bruised, perhaps damaged, but still warm and true. They had lived through the joys, the hard and sometimes dangerous work, and all the meetings, arguments, bitter disappointments, threats, and punishments that were part of being on the radical left in America from the thirties through the fifties. When they were young, they rallied to the cause of economic justice, racial equality, and the building of broad-based industrial unions to secure workers' rights. And Chicago, with its railroads, steel mills, and manufacturing plants, as well as its throngs of factory workers and Eastern European, Mexican, and black poor and working-class communities, was an obvious, almost perfect place to do the work.

At the time, I didn't think there was anything odd about how I grew up. I just assumed other Jewish parents were at least a little mixed-up with organized crime, that they had also inadvertently shared stories with their kids about how their friends used to work in a union, or teach at a school, but how those friends didn't really have a lot of choice about whether or not to continue that work. I assumed other thirteen-year-olds stayed up late to hear the nomination fight during the 1952 Republican Party convention, and then tried to join the ACLU like I did. Didn't everybody get lessons on how many different ways there were to be Jewish? To be a person? To be a grown-up?

Through my family and their friends, I was learning particular ways of looking at the world and how it works, who the good guys and bad guys were, who were winners and losers, and a little bit about why that was so. It was a political perspective, and it offered a way to make sense of the things I read about in the newspapers and saw myself. Perhaps even more critically, I learned that people I knew—family friends—had worked to change the world; that perhaps the world could and should be changed, and that maybe I could join in making those changes happen when I grew up.

My education wasn't just political, however. When I was seven or eight, my aunt Sadelle gave me *The Black Stallion* to read when I was stuck in bed with the measles. I became hooked on reading. How I loved it! Though I never finished all the books in Walter Farley's series, before too long I was reading some of the novels my mother still had from her days in college. Hemingway, Faulkner, and Fitzgerald all offered me windows into different, more entrancing worlds than the one I was living in. Private reading was then, and always would be, my alternative to whatever was supposed to be going on in schoolrooms.

I loved comic books, too. I preferred Batman, who seemed more real, more possible to me than Superman did. With enough training and determination, you could be Batman if you wanted to be. I read *Classic Comics* of course, and I collected *Tales from the Crypt*. *Mad* magazine also taught me new and very odd ways to look at the world.

Overall, I was growing up in a pretty typical working-class/ lower middle-class neighborhood in the city. When I started at South Shore High School in 1953, it was filled with mostly Jewish kids, and even the kids who weren't Jewish had gone to elementary schools with lots of Jewish kids, so the school's culture was dominated by my striving, college-focused peers.

I didn't intend to, but I slowly and casually moved away from what people thought I should be doing. I didn't want to join the overly earnest and dreary "clubs" that were organized around different academic subjects. I didn't want to work on the school newspaper, the *Shore Line*, or with the group that put out the *Tide*, the school yearbook. Instead, I watched what went on and learned that the boundaries of what you could get away with without getting into really serious trouble were further out than most people thought they were. I asked funny or snidely smart questions in class, and I didn't do all of the homework. The worst things that happened were slightly lower grades or not getting asked to join a high school fraternity. But there were always a number of other guys who also didn't wear the frat jackets and who I could hang out on a street corner and smoke with.

In 1955, the summer before I turned sixteen, though, I saw firsthand an injustice so obvious and cruel that it was impossible to ignore. It would affect the course of my life. In June, my mother and father announced the family would be taking a road trip to Canada. I didn't want to go. I said I'd rather use some of the money I had saved from odd jobs around the neighborhood to go by bus to New Orleans on my own. I don't know why New Orleans became a destination for me—maybe it was my mother's Faulkner novels or my father's stories about his Sephardic family members who lived there. For whatever reason, my parents were okay with this plan. So I took a Greyhound headed south. I remember the Mississippi River surging in a wide channel in St. Louis, the moss hanging from the trees that lined the long roads in Louisiana, and the French Quarter, where nobody even cared if I was a young kid having a drink at the bar and watching near-naked women dance around on a stage.

But what helped change my life on the trip was something that happened between St. Louis and Memphis. At one point, and without a word from anyone, when we were about to cross the Tennessee state line, every black passenger on the bus got up and quietly moved to seats in the back.

I was stunned. I had heard about Jim Crow laws, and had probably even talked about them on an earlier car trip my family had taken to Miami. I also lived in Chicago, where racial segregation by neighborhood was a given. But to see people I had been talking with and sitting next to suddenly become different people, degraded and set apart, was unexpected and wrenching. I was hit in the face with something real and ugly in America.

I didn't say a word. I stared out the window as the bus continued driving on and thought and brooded and seethed and felt too young and weak to do anything. But that acquiescence to evil and power—and my anger about it— stayed with me forever.

The job I got when I returned to Chicago taught me about hard living. I worked for a family friend who had a garage and gas station around Woodlawn and Sixty-Third Street. The Jews who had lived in the neighborhood earlier had almost completely moved out, replaced mostly by African American families. Many stores on Sixty-Third, however, were still owned and operated by Jews.

So I worked there pumping gas, learning from the two black employees how to fix flat tires, grease cars, and change oil. I learned how to drink hard liquor from a pint bottle in a paper bag; how to mix it with Coke; where to buy and how to use a switchblade knife; and how to be careful with the brown paper bags of slips or money that the numbers guys sometimes left in their cars.

At school I was getting more comfortable with being different. I carried a switchblade in the pocket of my Levi's jeans; it made me feel a little tougher and more grown-up than the other kids I knew. Because of the knife, I was also a little careless about where and when I walked. I had a few confrontations with kids from the rougher South Chicago neighborhood that curled around the eastern edges of Seventy-Ninth Street, a sometimes blurry boundary on the southern fringe of my own South Shore neighborhood. I was pretending to be tough, but I was also scared to death.

Eventually I started a small gambling operation. In an industrial art class one semester, where the desks were tall and wide with large pull-out drawers, I ran a "Twenty-Six" game out of one of the drawers. Twenty-Six is a Chicago-born dice game—you pick a number between one and six and roll dice out of a cup a set number of times, mostly trying to get the number you picked to show up twenty-six times. Few students at South Shore High knew they should be throwing the dice out of the cup thirteen times instead of the ten I allowed, so I made out pretty well with that game.

Around the same time, a far more consequential moment in my high school life occurred. Like all the other Jewish kids, I took physics my junior year. After that, everybody would take chemistry and the advanced math classes and then we'd all go to college to become doctors or lawyers.

At the end of the first week in physics, we had a quiz. I hadn't been paying attention in class, so I just leaned over toward the smart kid sitting next to me and copied all of his answers. When the tests were handed back on Monday, I got a terrifically good grade. As I looked at the returned test and then at the rest of the kids in the class, I knew that many of them worked much harder in school than I did. And I realized I didn't want to make whatever changes in my life would have been necessary to be as hardworking as they were and to compete with them for better grades in physics.

My life was already a little different than theirs. I had traveled on my own to faraway cities. I had learned things working at the gas station that other kids at South Shore hadn't. And the gambling operation had won me real money. I valued those experiences and saw them as concrete proof that I could do things differently, and I didn't want to work hard in school and grow up to be a doctor or lawyer. I wasn't sure what I wanted, but I was beginning to figure out what I didn't.

After staring at the returned test for a while, I got up and went to the front of the room and told the teacher I wasn't going to take physics. Then I walked right out of the class to the principal's office on the first floor and changed my class schedule. That was the year I took Commercial Law.

I had certainly left the aspiring middle-class Jewish boy track. If I'd been paying any kind of attention, it would already have been obvious that I wasn't going to necessarily take the expected path to adulthood that my friends were. All of it helped confirm my feelings that maybe I was different from most of the kids I knew, a notion that would slowly grow—as much in self-defense as it did for any other reason—into a core part of who I thought I was. And that frustrating, scary, and proud sense of difference surely helped provide an important base upon which I could later build an alternative and very political sense of self.

But there wasn't a lot of political talk during my high school years. Some of the kids at South Shore High had parents who had either been caught up in or terrified by the communist-baiting repression, and perhaps because of that, the silence surrounding politics made some sense. Maybe some of the neighborhood kids didn't exactly know what their parents had gone through, and others knew enough to know it wasn't something you talked about. It might have been different in other neighborhoods, but I didn't know those places.

And the whole notion of a "neighborhood" as a definable place where people who were alike lived together apart from outsiders—so important and blatant in an ethnically and racially divided and sometimes violently segregated Chicago—was one of the hidden gifts of knowledge the city and my family gave me while I was growing up. It wasn't just black and white, rich and poor—America's divisions were way more complicated than that. Nothing the Marxists would tell me later about class warfare was any surprise at all. All of it was undeniably visible to me as a kid. Growing up, you saw and heard the subtle but important distinctions between people that couldn't be contained in introductory sociology courses, political slogans, or most political dreams. I didn't need a lecture or a book to understand a lot about America and where I was supposed to belong in it.

Chapter 2

Becoming a Political Radical

I didn't bother to take the SATs during my senior year of high school; my grades and the courses I took weren't going to be very attractive to any discerning college. The University of Illinois, however, had to accept you if you graduated with some fairly minimal grade point average or class rank, so that's where I went.

In college, I found new friends who hoped as I did that politics in America didn't have to be something you only talked about in a few classes or read about in the newspaper. There were kids whose parents had been Communist Party members, or had friends who had been, and they weren't embarrassed or frightened by it. I went to campus concerts by Pete Seeger with people who knew most of the words to the old union songs. There were conversations over coffee in the basement cafeteria of the Y that included laughter (and a little awe) about the actual Jewish names of all those old Bolsheviks.

The first real politics of my life started so slowly I barely noticed. I could probably still find the street a friend and I walked down in 1959, both of us just twenty, bemoaning the fact that we were too late for the union struggles, too late to fight fascism, too late for the revolution. Then in 1960, a biology professor at the university was quickly fired after the college newspaper published his letter that said "sufficiently mature" students who wouldn't be "violating their own moral code" could consider having premarital sex. Some of us didn't like that he was fired. It made no sense. We were a university and it was wrong and we should do something about it. There were hurried, small meetings in that basement cafeteria at the Y, and on "Moms Day," when parents were invited to visit campus, we decided to actually do something.

For the first time, I made use of the stories I had heard growing up. I got on top of a car with a bullhorn to disrupt the parade that was part of the Moms Day event and to mobilize support for the fired professor. It was the first time I knew that the police were paying enough attention to me to take my picture. Friends stole copies of the photos from the university's administrative offices and put them up, along with other photos of the demonstration, on the wall of the little coffeehouse/hot dog joint where we hung out. I laughed about it, but neither my mother nor father thought it was funny when I took them to see the photos during their visit to campus to be sure I wasn't in any trouble.

Later that year, things got more serious. The TV news continued reporting on the sit-ins in Greensboro and everywhere else. The same small group of students that had created the Moms Day protest began picketing at the local Woolworth's to support the sit-ins. As we walked up and down on the sidewalk, we could hope and even feel that life might be beginning to change.

Unknown to anybody I knew in Champaign-Urbana, that same spring the Students for a Democratic Society (SDS) had held its founding conference in Ann Arbor, Michigan. SDS was a national organization of activist students who were committed to supporting civil rights and progressive change in America. If we had known that we weren't as isolated at U of I as we seemed to be—surrounded by cornfields in the middle of nowhere—maybe I would have been more certain that what we were doing was more than just an exciting moment, some hopeful, brief effort to be part of something bigger, something political and important. But we didn't know.

By 1961, I was a senior and had gotten engaged to Adelle Katz, who I'd met in a summer school class at Navy Pier a couple of years before. She was from Rogers Park, then a mostly working-class Jewish neighborhood on the city's North Side, and seeing her meant schlepping up to parts of the city I had barely ever visited before. She had joined me in Champaign in the fall. Although I was beginning to find ways to be political on campus, Adelle hadn't come from the same overtly political family background that I was grounded in, and she wasn't particularly interested in such things. She wasn't opposed to them, but it was more important for her to do well in school and get her degree. Her father had long ago worked as a furrier making coats at some large company; he'd lost his job and his career as a consequence of a failed labor union strike. I was sure that Adelle's determination to get her degree grew in part out of seeing her own father's years long scramble for work to support his family.

By the time Adelle and I were engaged, our families were satisfied we were doing what they anticipated. I'd been admitted to the University of Chicago's grad school that coming fall and was moving with a friend into a shared apartment in the city. To alter the direction my life was taking then, I would have needed more certainty that those hints at political change that I had experienced in college were serious and real. Instead, in the spring of 1961, I graduated and just went along as if my immediate world was the only world that counted, and my plans about marriage and graduate school still made perfect sense.

Before graduate school started, I got a job as a case worker for Chicago's Welfare Department on Sixty-Third Street off the corner of Cottage Grove. It was a harsher part of the same deteriorating South Side neighborhood under the "L" tracks where I had worked years before pumping gas. In the short time that had gone by, the street seemed shabbier, dirtier, and more crowded. The two- and three-story buildings, with their storefronts hard up against the sidewalks on both sides of the street, were occasionally interrupted by empty windows that announced failed or vanished stores. Sometimes there was a new storefront church spread across two commercial spaces. There were still a few white store owners around, but I didn't see many of them, and most of the other white people I saw on the street were either cops, people rushing to get on or off the "L," or other welfare caseworkers.

Every day that summer, the work I did drove punishing truths into my head about what was wrong in America. While the people living in that neighborhood were usually and simply categorized as "poor and black," the reality of what I was thrown into was more accurately described as "a brutally imposed, punishing, hopeless degradation of people of color who didn't have enough money to live anything like a decent life." I became a poverty tourist who was wrapped up in bureaucratic rules and protections. Just a little north of Sixty-Third on Stoney Island Avenue, I visited a single mother and her baby, who were living in the converted coal bin or storage room in the basement of what had once been a fairly elegant multi-unit apartment building. Now the building surrounded three sides of a bare courtyard that was littered with the glass shards of broken bottles. I was there to confirm that this young mother was still in need of public assistance and that her child was being adequately cared for. I was supposed to write all my findings down in some growing collection of "field notes" in her "case record." I remember that her place was so small, so crowded with low-hanging pipes, jumbled furniture, and clothes, we had to talk together in the doorway—half in and half out of her place—because there was no room for me to step inside.

After checking in with that young mother and other families in the same building, I'd walk south a few blocks on

Stoney Island to do my "field visits" at what was supposed to be a transient hotel. There, in small, thin-walled subdivided rooms, I'd stand or sit on battered kitchen chairs and talk with other mothers and their children about food, medicine, rent, and whatever escape fantasies they had about returning boyfriends or the potential of more help from their own mothers and families. All the better things were always about to happen sometime soon.

What made these visits all the more gut-wrenching was that only a couple of short blocks north, you could find the block-wide grassy expanses of the Midway, stretching many long blocks east to west. The Midway was one of the remnants of the 1893 Chicago World's Fair that still dotted places on the South Side, especially near the lake. It had once held sideshows, including Ferris's Wheel and Buffalo Bill's Wild West Show. Now it was like a green moat that separated two worlds. One was desperately poor, oppressed, and black; the other comfortably middle-class, academic, and white. That other side, is where I went to grad school after the summer ended. Hyde Park and the University of Chicago were literally just a few blocks north of the horror, poverty, and desperation I had spent the summer drowning in. The separation between the two side-by-side neighborhoods was so blatant, so near absolute, that it was difficult to believe.

I studied sociology in damp, chilly classrooms that were housed in stone, faux-Gothic buildings separated by grassy walkways. I was bored and unhappy and couldn't quite recall why I had decided to go to graduate school. Still, in classes and walking around the campus, I met politically oriented people. I ended up listening to the Red Army Chorus, the Weavers, and old union songs on vinyl LPs in the ratty apartments of other grad students. I found YPSL, the Young People's Socialist League, and the Student Peace Union. The SPU, headquartered just off campus, was a modest collection of anti-nuclear war student groups that were scattered across dozens of colleges in the Midwest and Northeast; its black and white button pin with the Campaign for Nuclear Disarmament logo grew up to be the now fairly universal peace symbol. I also found CORE, the Congress of Racial Equality. All of these groups were part of the evolving, growing early wisps of a movement, being filled out with kids who had grown up in hard left families, but also with kids who had grown up like I did, in families where "politics" was simply one of a collection of important and readily available ways to describe and explain the world around us. There was nothing particularly exceptional about it; it was one more part of everyday life. Like having money or being smart or being Jewish, politics was just something else to keep in mind. So political explanations were available to us, and we all were still angry about the brutality and racism we had seen in every TV story about the sit-ins.

I stopped attending most of my classes and started going to more meetings. CORE had been recruiting people to join the Freedom Riders, who were taking buses together to challenge and confront segregation in southern cities. We had serious talks about how to respond to violence; lecturers offered introductory lessons about rolling into a ball and covering your head. At family lunches on Sundays in restaurants in Chicago's gentrifying Old Town neighborhood, my father told me I'd never get a real job if I kept getting more involved with the things I was talking about, the things my friends and I were slowly, mostly hopefully, were beginning to call "the Movement." My mother tried to be understanding, but she was very ambivalent. The goals were right, but why couldn't I just get an advanced degree and teach in a college somewhere?

I recognized her concerns. Too many of her old friends had been crushed in internal Communist Party struggles. Theirs was a political life filled with heartache over lost hopes and dreams. None of this was ever said to me directly, but I was expected to understand that my mother wanted to protect me from all that pain. Probably in response to my mother's concerns, my grandfather, as a belated wedding present in early 1962, suddenly decided to send me to Israel for a year to study at the Hebrew University in Jerusalem. I accepted the gift, even though I knew it was the family's way to get me back to my Jewish roots and away from the possibility of riding buses into strange and dangerous southern cities or some other craziness.

My family's decision to shield me from politics by sending me to Israel backfired spectacularly. I studied political philosophy, met Jewish and Arab members of their Communist Party, visited *kibbutzim* and Arab villages, and talked politics endlessly. I met and became friends with Jerry Rubin, who would become a major political activist in America in just a few years, and I became more convinced that radical changes were needed in America.

Jerry was in Israel with his younger brother Gil, escaping the grasp of family after their parents had died; their family, like mine, saw Israel as an acceptable place to be outside of America. While Adelle was enrolled at Bezalel, the national art school, learning how to be a potter, spinning clay and experimenting with heat and color, Jerry and I were trying to figure out what the world was really like and who we wanted to be. We'd ride out to the university together on my Vespa and take buses to the desert or a socialist *kibbutz*.

Back then, Jerusalem was a city still physically divided by the outcome of the 1948 War of Independence. (I didn't hear the alternative way of describing that conflict—*nakba* in Arabic, *catastrophe* in English—until years later.) When Adelle and I went to the King David Hotel to have iced coffee on the outdoor back patio, we could look over toward East Jerusalem and see the barren ground and a few ruined small structures between the two halves of the city. The former brick factory where my wife did most of her pottery work was right up against the border, and there were two army tanks in the courtyard facing east toward a high brick wall that surrounded the factory grounds on three sides—"just in case" is how I always thought of it when I visited Adelle there. Driving the Vespa back up the hills to Jerusalem after a visit in Tel Aviv, we'd pass several burned out, rusted armored vehicles that were pushed over to the side of the road, but still kept there as reminders of war. And there was a place where the road swerved to the left and up, away from a rough patch of level ground that led toward the border with Jordan, which was not very far away at all from the two-lane highway we drove on.

It was in Jerusalem that I first saw a child with flies in his eyes. The *ulpan*, the Hebrew language school we went to when we first arrived in Israel, was in a moderately poor neighborhood. Living nearby were much poorer Moroccan Jews who were newly arrived in Israel. It was a very young Moroccan Jewish child I saw listlessly sitting on the curb as I walked back toward the *ulpan* from Zion Square, where we had learned you could get the best falafel sandwiches from an old man who cooked them on a street corner cart. I didn't know how to respond when I saw that child. I had read about such a thing, and half-remembered seeing pictures of people suffering and enduring small swarms of flies near their faces. But to see it in Jerusalem, in a Jewish child's eyes with no one immediately caring or attending to him, was almost unbelievable; I wanted to do something to help, to change the life that child was living that kept him vulnerable to such a horror. But it wasn't my country. I was only a temporary visitor, and I finally just continued walking back to the *ulpan*. The image of that child, though, was burned into my memory. I set it alongside the images of other instances of need, cruelty, and injustice—from the sit-ins in the South to the Chicago streets around Sixty-Third. These pictures in my mind made me angry, and I was ever more determined that I had to do something about such ugliness and pain.

After a little more than a year in Israel, Adelle and I returned to America, and I chose to go to grad school in social work. It seemed the easiest and fastest way to get some of the practical lessons, concrete information, and experiences I thought I might need to help people work together and create the real changes in America I was now certain were required. So I enrolled at Loyola, where I learned how to listen, how to more consistently and carefully and appropriately support people to be stronger. After getting my degree in 1965, I joined up with the Mayor's Commission on Youth Welfare to work both with kids in trouble and with the cops in a very rough part of Chicago on the Near North Side, west of the gentrifying Wells Street restaurants, away from the lake and the parks and the Gold Coast wealth, in neighborhoods dominated by poor and African American families.

The kids we worked with might have had a couple of minor run-ins with the cops, or maybe one of our gang workers had bumped into a kid on the streets and sent them our way. Neighbors might call the mayor's office to say they thought some family or kid was in trouble, and we'd go out to see what was going on. It was one of those well-intended "outreach experiments" based on emerging social work theories about how to help kids and families in poor neighborhoods by providing "comprehensive" and "coordinated" services from local offices. Even in theory, and especially in practice in Chicago, the theory regretfully accepted that it couldn't do much of anything except soften some of the cruelest edges of wealth inequality, poverty, racism, and political power that were the real drivers of the pain and hurt I saw every day.

The Cabrini-Green public housing project, off both sides of Division Street, was part of our territory. The buildings that once made it up are all torn down now. Cabrini-Green started in 1942 as a low-rise, racially mixed community with grassy yards and playgrounds for poor and working-class families. But Chicago's citywide pattern of racially segregated housing, along with the job losses that accompanied the closing of the neighborhood's factories and warehouses in the postwar years, had destroyed all that. By the time I was working in the neighborhood, Cabrini-Green was only made up of black families who lived in stark, immense, deteriorating buildings with yards that had been paved over to reduce maintenance costs. The twenty-three towers, which were called "vertical ghettos," had 3,000 apartments and more than 20,000 residents.

By 1965, Cabrini-Green already had a reputation as a harsh, dangerous place, but it seemed to me then that the neighborhood's reputation was a little worse than the place actually was. The different gangs didn't yet dominate their individual buildings, guns weren't everywhere, and young kids still played in the broad open spaces between the buildings. But it was still ugly and threatening. You watched out for who might be in the elevator with you because violent robberies and beatings in those enclosed spaces weren't uncommon. If there were small groups of tough kids I didn't know hanging around, or if the mothers I spoke with on the playgrounds seemed worried about something they weren't quite willing to talk about, then I'd want to have someone meet me downstairs to accompany me up to the apartments.

The ratty offices we worked out of were above some storefronts near the corner of Division and Orleans, across from the police precinct station and about a half mile east of the public housing projects. Every so often, I rode with youth officers in their cars, cruising the streets where I was supposed to help them "work more effectively with" the kids they stopped and hassled. In that part of the city back then, only a few of the kids had guns, though a great many of the ones I knew had a friend with a gun or carried knives themselves. But all the kids I worked with, their parents, and all the owners of the small corner stores I knew, agreed with the cops that I was probably the only unarmed white boy in the neighborhood.

Unfortunately, I didn't fit in with the Youth Welfare Office or their mission to help one kid at a time with the limited list of resources that were available. I spent too much time on the streets and in the kids' homes and not enough time writing reports. The more I worked, the more the entire operation seemed a useless fantasy.

One night, in the middle of one of Chicago's classic, drenching, late-summer thunderstorms, we were all called out to do an emergency sweep of the neighborhoods to get in touch with kids we knew. There had been some report or rumor of impending gang violence. I was paired with one of our agency's gang workers. That night he chose to wear a sports jacket, and I assumed that meant he'd decided to arm himself before going out. We drove a bit, walked a lot, and talked to anyone we found on the street. Then we drove somewhere else and then walked even more. We were out for hours. By the time we staggered back into the office, we were soaked through. Without really thinking about it, I grabbed a handful of the Chicago city flag that was hanging on an upright pole next to the door where we walked in (the American flag was on another pole). I quickly wiped my face off and began our report to the gathered senior staff and commanding police officers. But people weren't listening. Instead, everyone in the room was glaring at me. My boss shouted furiously that if it had been the American flag I had used to wipe my face, "I would have shot you right here and now, you son of a bitch." I nearly quit that night and was surely getting close to being fired.

Thankfully, soon after that I got an opportunity to do the real work I wanted and needed to do. Turns out that being seen walking on the streets day and night and hanging out and talking to the kids and their families meant I was establishing a reputation. I was offered the chance to be a community organizer in the same neighborhood, with a small salary and support from the local settlement house. The group I'd work with was called The United Friends—"TUF." I can't claim the creative brilliance behind that acronym, which I loved from the beginning. That honor likely goes to Dottie Palombo. Dottie was a tall redhead from South Carolina, tough as nails and so smart. More than any SDS friends, she taught me how to survive and be the organizer I wanted to become. I helped people in the neighborhood come together to identify what was hurting them and to figure out what they needed and wanted to do to fight back effectively. This included spray-painting signs on abandoned or totally neglected buildings, declaring they were now a "TUF Project;" helping to start Welfare and Tenant Unions, the Legal Aid clinic, and Co-op Food Buying clubs; and fighting to create new affordable housing without displacing people in the current neighborhood. There were loud raucous demonstrations against slum landlords and the city that let them flourish. We took trash from vacant lots and basements and filled the alcove in front of one landlord's storefront office. At the city offices in the Loop, we dumped rats and roaches into the reflecting pool beside the huge Picasso sculpture. There were occasional arrests of course, but no one was ever held for too long. And the arrests were generally done calmly, with everybody on both sides understanding that they shouldn't behave too roughly. The only excitement usually came from bystanders who sometimes grew a little too enthusiastic in their support for either the cops or us.

One of the very first group arrests landed us in the local precinct lockup, where I knew some of the cops from my earlier work with the Mayor's Commission on Youth Welfare. That turned out to be a very good thing. We were milling around in the large holding cell, waiting to be processed, when one of the people who had joined us in dumping trash in front of a landlord's office came to me and said he had a problem. He was an older guy, and he told me he had a gun in his pocked because he'd forgotten to leave it at home. I agreed that was definitely a problem. I called over to one of the cops in the corridor, found out that I knew the desk sergeant on duty, and asked to have him come down to speak with me privately while I was still locked up. Before too long, I was leaning up against the front cell wall, and the sergeant who had remembered me was leaning on the cell bars on the other side. We looked like we were just having a friendly chat, but he quickly agreed that nobody needed the kind of problem I explained we might have. Eventually, I got the guy's pistol into my pocket and came back over to the desk sergeant. I slipped it between the bars to him as quickly and unobtrusively as possible. That was the last anybody heard about it.

This was in 1966, and neither the police sergeant nor I recognized at the time that we were playing out parts in the fading remnants of a Chicago where mutually self-restrained, local interactions sometimes occurred between demonstrators and the police. Demonstrators were becoming angrier and more determined, and the police were only beginning to understand the growing threat that change represented to their absolute power and authority on the streets.

TUF also started a federally chartered credit union—one of the first credit unions open to anybody within a neighborhood's physical boundaries rather than to a more formal collection of people (like members of a labor union). In addition to all the paperwork, setting up the credit union, because it might be seen as a threat to the loan sharking operations on the street, required a late afternoon personal meeting at a ratty bar on Sedgwick. It involved a couple of our guys and a couple mob guys who were involved with moneylending at some of the neighborhood's few remaining industrial plants.

We had to work out a truce; we wouldn't offer credit union membership to any of the white workers on their turf, and they wouldn't hassle us for recruiting black workers. Everybody else at the meeting was drinking beer, but I was drinking whiskey because I'm allergic to beer. The bar was on the rough west edge of what was then the emerging, gentrified "Old Town" restaurant row. We were practically the only people in the place, except for a young folk singer up on a low, small stage who was playing a little too loudly while we were all trying to talk. I caught the singer's name, Arlo Guthrie, and it pissed me off because I didn't think he could sing very well. Besides, I thought he was probably just taking advantage of his father's name, which I knew well from all those union songs I'd heard in college. Due to the mix of whiskey and my worry about the deal we were trying to make, I went up and told him to get the hell off the stage. He quickly scurried away.

While my first personal encounter with sixties music wasn't so terrific, the community organizing work seemed to be going great. The Welfare Union, which was composed of single mothers struggling to survive while maintaining their dignity and self-respect, was growing. One early recruit lived around the corner and down the street, just a block or so from TUF's storefront, so she was easy to find and talk to. She was a big woman—tall, full-bodied, and pretty tough. At one of the meetings where we planned things like going as a group to the welfare office to confront some particularly nasty caseworker, she asked whether she could bring her mother to the next meeting. The next week she did. Her mother was small, thin, and to my young, barely experienced eyes, a much older woman. But like her daughter, she was tough. This wasn't anywhere near the first time she had joined with others to fight against the city and for people who were poor. She told me about other meetings when she was younger, when the Cabrini low-rise row houses were newly built and the neighborhood was still racially mixed. Despite the war, people joined together—including some of the workers from the factories that then dotted major streets—to demand better schools, better upkeep of the row houses, and higher wages. It all rang some bells in my head, and sure enough, when I checked with two of my mother's friends who had been in the Party, they confirmed that that neighborhood, so close to the wealth of the Gold Coast, and with factories and poor white and black families living together, had been a prime place to recruit and organize.

On freezing winter nights, sitting on cheap metal folding chairs around the large, plastic-topped tables, there were two generations who had fought and were still fighting to have their worth as human beings recognized and valued, people trying to force the city they lived in to offer the protections and help they needed. I was learning important lessons. It almost certainly was going to take more time than we hoped to make the changes that needed to be made in our country. It might even take generations. But people's determination to resist and fight back against injustice couldn't be underestimated. And a big part of me assumed that the young kids who sometimes came with their mothers to the meetings, or sometimes on our group visits to the welfare offices, would be a next generation in that same struggle.

Movement organizers—practically all of us young, white, and college educated—were everywhere in the city then. Because the national SDS offices were in Chicago, I met lots of people like me, all of us working on the streets in different cities, working hard to make America better. In those days we dreamed American dreams—economic justice, the end of racism—and nearly all of us believed we could help make those dreams come true.

It was clear, however, that the movement I was part of was changing fast. Ending the war in Vietnam began to overwhelm everything. My old friend from Israel, Jerry Rubin, had become a committed anti-war activist and publicly recognized leader in the Berkeley-San Francisco efforts against the war. He and other political friends would visit the shabby storefront office of the community organization where I proudly worked on the corner of Cleveland and Evergreen. They couldn't understand why there weren't any multicolored flyers announcing some demonstration against the war alongside the co-op food shopping list handouts that were piled up on tables near the front door. They weren't very forgiving about it either. They argued that fighting to stop the war was the most important thing that could be done—it had to have the greatest priority for our work. It symbolized everything wrong in the country. It was an immediately threatening and recognizable evil that had to be stopped.

But the people I worked with in those shattered buildings and urine-stained hallways were not focused on the war in Vietnam. They wanted my help to wage war against a city that never listened to them, against absentee landlords who collected rents and never cleared away the garbage, against schools that failed to educate their children, and against a welfare system that degraded them. They were fighting a war against all the political lies and false promises they faced every day.

I was then, and still am, terribly biased toward wanting to work directly to change America. I know the unjust wars our country wages must be resisted. I understand that those violent aggressions are almost always a visible, ugly expression of an American politics and economy that are dangerous. I know, despite all the hopeful language—and even the occasional good intentions—that those aggressions will almost certainly punish people rather than protect them. But in my own life, I've worked harder and longer to combat racism, poverty, bigotry, and powerlessness here in America. And years ago, when I took one of my children on a visit to Chicago and we drove down Cleveland Avenue, I proudly showed off the well-designed townhouses that The United Friends had been able to build without displacing too many neighbors.

In the summer of 1967, the violence in cities like Detroit and Newark was being faintly but clearly echoed on the streets I was walking. There was an overwhelming sense of the near certainty of similar violence in Chicago's black neighborhoods. The true explosion of rage wouldn't happen until April 1968, after the assassination of Martin Luther King, when snipers began firing day and night from the upper floors of Cabrini-Green. But the threat and anticipation of that violence effectively closed off almost any hope of continuing my work. America no longer seemed willing or capable of simply being persuaded to change for the better, or even being shown how it could be better. Something more radical was necessary.

Add that collapse of hope and meaningful work to the escalating war in Vietnam and the rising resistance to that war on campuses and in the streets, and whatever tenuous faith I and my friends might have had in gradual progress towards social justice in America dribbled away to almost nothing. Creating real change would require something else, something more. SDS leader Rennie Davis had already left for full-time anti-war work from the SDS-sponsored "Jobs or Income Now" (JOIN) community organization that was working with white, southern migrants in Chicago's Uptown neighborhood. Another SDS leader, Mike James, would soon enough leave the same project to work on the more explicitly "revolutionary organization and newspaper," *Rising Up Angry*.

In the long-distance arguments I had on the phone with Jerry about what I should be doing politically, I wasn't able to defend my work anymore. He told me that even SDS founder Tom Hayden, who had been working as a community organizer in Newark, had to leave and that "he wanted to anyway," that half the people we knew who used to be with

SDS were either engaged in anti-war activities or hanging around the Bay area or the Lower East Side doing dope and trying to figure out how to fight against the war and create something totally different in their own lives. "Come to New York," he'd say, "then you'll see." So I went and visited Jerry, who had left behind his straighter anti-war persona and had enthusiastically joined the emerging counterculture of music, dope, and imaginative political protest on Manhattan's Lower East Side. He introduced me to a funny, smart, and welcoming new friend of his named Abbie Hoffman.

Abbie was almost impossible not to like—at least most of the time. He had long, untamed hair and a joyful, full-faced smile. He had worked in the South and then run a battered storefront on the Lower East Side that sold handicrafts from rural southern families to support the Student Nonviolent Coordinating Committee (SNCC). His enthusiastic engagement with different pieces of the alternative culture— from music to free food to the phone phreaks' blue boxes (which imitated the electronic tones of a dialed phone so you could make free calls) to weed and acid—often made him seem less hard-edged politically. But he was always political.

Abbie in those days was vibrant, aglow with energy and political wit and satire in the service of changing America and ending the war. He had a genuine ebullience and ease that Jerry didn't. He always seemed to strain less than Jerry did, and he fit more easily into the alternative counterculture universe of music, long hair, drugs, swirling bright colors, radical politics, and streets crowded with young people in cities and college towns around the country.

I had no notion of just how consequential those early meeting with Jerry and Abbie and their very often stoned but sparkling, smart, and inventive friends would be to my life. At first it was just something new, a different, privately joyful way to talk and think about politics with people who were easy and fun to be with. Poets like Allen Ginsberg, who I'd read, now joined in dinners with everybody else, and the political conversations and plans begin to feel a little more real. Everybody got high, and we crowded into the balcony seats at the Fillmore East to listen to music and watch the light show. After the concerts, I surely hoped, but never truly believed, that the political fantasies and the much more serious talk would actually help change America and my life. But they did.

Chapter 3

Taking to the Streets

Soon enough it was clear that it really made no sense for me to continue working in the Cabrini-Green community. Large-scale, more substantial changes were needed. And besides, my white face was increasingly a liability (if not quite yet a full source of resentment) in the neighborhood. I decided to go back to graduate school, this time at Northwestern, in sociology again. But now I had a very specific notion of what I wanted to study: the theory and practices of how ordinary citizens were transformed into professional revolutionaries. If we had to prepare to do things differently to create the changes in America we all believed in, maybe we could learn from how others had changed their lives and then the politics of other countries. I spent time trying to figure out how people went from being isolated, angry, frightened, beaten-down individuals living in a particular place and time to being an organized revolutionary force. I thought about Moses and his recruitment of Aaron to help break the Israelites out of Egypt. I read about how Loyola set up his Jesuits to fight back against the Reformation. I looked a lot more closely at how some of those old Bolsheviks became who they were.

Now free of the day-to-day obligations of a community organizer, I also started traveling to New York more often to hang out with Jerry and Abbie and so many other wonderfully odd and interesting people who were committed to political and cultural change. I smoked more dope than usual, and I listened to everybody talking, arguing, laughing, and trying hard to figure out what came next in our politics.

My research and thinking about how people transformed themselves into professional revolutionaries made it easy for me to agree when Jerry and a few other people asked me to help with the anti-war demonstration they were planning for that coming summer during the Democratic National Convention in Chicago. The invitation to help wasn't based on anything much. I lived in Chicago, so I'd likely be there when they might need some help. A lot of the things people were talking about doing during the demonstrations would likely happen in the parks and streets in the Near North Side neighborhoods I had worked in. Nobody was quite sure of the kind of help they might need, but I had known Jerry forever, and I got along with Abbie, so why not? And it wasn't much of a commitment on my part, mostly just nodding my head in agreement.

I had never been involved in national demonstrations before. In the local demonstrations I had either planned or joined, all the organizing work and the rough and tumble of the demonstrations themselves were all contained within limited physical boundaries: a small number of city blocks, or a particular building or office on a certain street. All of them were usually conducted without much press coverage and between antagonists—police and demonstrators—who often enough had some familiarity with each other because of earlier, small-scale, neighborhood demonstrations and the occasional arrest.

The demonstrations at the Democratic National Convention were going to be very different. By the summer of 1968, the world had changed, raising the stakes we were all playing for. In late January and through much of February, the Tet Offensive in Vietnam was on the national news every night, impossible to ignore. The war was worse than anybody had ever acknowledged. Sometime earlier, in the fall or early winter of 1967, Abbie had called me, joyfully demanding that

I immediately get a color television set. "It's fucking amazing!" he screamed. "CBS is doing our work for us!" Watching the flames and fallen soldiers and slaughtered civilians in the Tet news reports on our new color TV, I was certain he was right.

In early March, the insurgent McCarthy campaign unexpectedly won 42 percent of the vote in the New Hampshire Democratic presidential primary, nearly upsetting the president, Lyndon B. Johnson. Four days later, Robert Kennedy entered the race for the nomination. On March 31, President Johnson withdrew his candidacy, declaring he would neither seek nor accept the Democratic nomination for president. Less than a week later, Martin Luther King was killed, and by the next night, fire and rage and looting and death spread across many American cities. In Chicago, blocks of the black neighborhoods on the West Side burned, and shops and stores were looted. Nine people were killed by the police and National Guard.

Toward the end of a week of violence on the city streets, after things seemed to be calming down, Mayor Daley publicly and dramatically announced an order to the police: "shoot to kill arsonists" and "shoot to maim looters." That announcement scared everybody I knew who was still working in the already struggling community organizations around the city. It also scared people who might have been thinking of coming to Chicago to protest during the convention. People would later say they decided not to come because the mayor had made it clear he would violently punish anybody in his city who did anything he didn't like.

On June 6, Robert Kennedy was assassinated. Many people who had been clinging to remnants of hope for visible, positive change in America and an end to the war through electoral politics sank into an abyss. The McCarthy people, who had invested so much in what had seemed such a hopeless but necessary enterprise, held on to their hope that the election would still make a difference. There were also those who supported Hubert Humphrey, remembering the liberal politician he had been before he became vice president, and who they believed he might be again once he was freed from the constraints of the Johnson administration's war.

My reactions to Robert Kennedy's assassination were terribly mixed. I was stunned and horrified at another Kennedy killing, and I was thrown back to the memories of being frozen for days in front of the TV when his brother was murdered. But the killing confirmed my worst fears about America's existing political system; that it might never be able to honestly confront and respond to the hurts caused by the war, poverty, and racism. It was clear to me that the demonstrations, and the work against the war and American political and economic power, had to continue and had to grow.

There were two different groups planning mass protests at the Democratic National Convention. The first was the Mobilization to End the War in Vietnam, or the "Mobe," a broad-based traditional collection of anti-war activists, leftist organizations, and peace groups that for years had spearheaded all the local and national protests against the war and mobilized thousands of people in marches, demonstrations, and occasional nonviolent public acts of resistance against the government and the corporations whose work supported the war. It was headed by Dave Dellinger, a lifelong pacifist and anti-war activist, and two former SDS leaders, Tom Hayden and Rennie Davis, who I knew from earlier encounters in Chicago. Then there were my new friends on New York's Lower East Side who had publicly morphed into the "Youth International Party," or the "Yippies." They had announced a "Festival of Life," a counterculture alternative to the Mobe demonstrations. Abbie promised free music, poetry, free food, and a chance to show an alternative way of life to the warmongering politicians, and Jerry asked "Marxist acidheads" and "psychedelic Bolsheviks" to come to Chicago to enjoy the music and join the protests.

My early work for the Democratic National Convention protests involved connecting the people I knew, who were still struggling to maintain the remnants of community organizing work in Chicago, to the demonstrations. The local organizers weren't happy; they were certain the demonstrations would bring untold troubles from the police into their communities. I brought Jerry and Abbie to meetings with some of those local organizers to try to make nice, but it didn't work out well. Most of the local folks did not like either the Mobe or the Yippies who were then separately planning protests. The only people who reluctantly accepted the fact that the demonstrations were going to happen and that they had to try to find some way to help were members of the proto-hippie community clustered around Chicago's underground newspaper, *The Seed*, on the Near North Side.

By mid-August, it was clear the city would not give anybody permits that might help make traditional protest marches and political demonstrations more doable. They weren't going to allow any grand music festival, and demonstrators couldn't sleep in the city parks. And there weren't going to be near the number of people showing up in Chicago that we had hoped for. The lack of permits and the city's threats against protesters effectively combined to stop people who might otherwise have come. It was also clear that acting like the Mobe and Yippie efforts were somehow actually separate from one another made no sense at all. The Mobe had an office in an old building in the Loop; that's where they held meetings, made plans, talked strategy and tactics, and issued press releases. The Yippies mostly hung out around some donated street level space near Lincoln Park, painted signs to hang up in the park to help people find their way to free food and music, and played provocative, sly, or outrageous verbal games with the growing collection of press and TV people who were always looking for a story. But on the days leading up to convention week, the only noticeable action—excepting the recurring and always losing tussles in courtrooms over permits—was in Lincoln Park. There the differences between the Mobe and Yippies were more about clothes and hair length. Everybody was just together, hanging out on the grass, wandering around, talking, and waiting for something to start.

Since the Yippies didn't work too hard at actually organizing anything, and because my politics back then almost always required me to have specific tasks to do, I went to some of the Mobe meetings. Because I knew a thing or two about Chicago and the streets, knew Rennie from his earlier community organizing days in the city, and was not obviously crazy or too young, I ended up helping in the tactical training of the "marshals," the kids who showed up early in Chicago and who would help shepherd and protect the crowds during the convention protests.

Early on I met and paired up with a long-haired, bearded, Yippie named Wolfe Lowenthal who had more actual training and experience in physical self-defense than I did. We helped in the intermittent and comically ineffective efforts to organize protesters in the park to practice "snake dances," something Japanese students used to break through police lines, moving in unison, shouting "*Wa'shoi! Wa'shoi!*"—left, right, left, right. We might not have had much hope of actually using such a tactic to protect demonstrators in Chicago, but the news cameras loved it. Somewhat more seriously, though we were still a little doubtful about its practicality, we taught the kids to use rolled up magazines—I remember using an issue of *Ramparts*—to hold up in two hands to block a policeman's downward swinging club, a weapon we definitely expected the cops to use against the demonstrators.

J. Anthony Lukas of the *New York Times* interviewed me during that pre-convention week, and he quoted me as saying:

> obviously things are going to be getting rough here. We've got to be prepared . . . We're still dedicated to peaceful methods, but I can tell you there are some doubts in the movement these days about the old-time nonviolent stance—you know, rolling yourself up in a little ball . . . and getting clubbed. Some of the guys who've done that have been very badly hurt . . . We're planning some more active and mobile forms of self-defense.

From the earliest planning for the Chicago convention protests, everyone was alert to the likelihood that the city and its police would do everything it could to delay, prevent, minimize, and punish political demonstrations against the Democrats and the war. And while I might have hoped that things wouldn't get truly terrible on the streets, it was a fragile hope.

I was in the park on Friday, August 23, with the convention scheduled to start on Monday, still trying to help the marshals prepare for what was coming, when down in the Loop, Jerry and a small group of other Yippies, including Wolfe, introduced Pigasus, the live pig they intended to nominate for president. Many were arrested somewhat peacefully, but Abbie loudly declared that if the pig and the Yippies weren't freed, they'd bring in a lion to run for president.

On the Saturday before the convention, the park began to fill up a little more, mainly with young people, but also with straighter looking, somewhat older guys everybody assumed were undercover cops. Things stayed relaxed, though, and if the crowd still wasn't as large as we'd hoped, the day was pleasant enough. But that night, a little past the 11:00 p.m. curfew, cops came in on three-wheeled motorcycles or walking in small skirmish lines. They moved fairly slowly and without much apparent malice to clear everybody out, and they stopped their efforts when they reached the park's outer perimeter. Allen Ginsberg led a fair-sized group of people out toward the west; I walked south out of the park with other folks to where I had parked my car. Driving back to my apartment, I remember thinking, "that wasn't so bad." But I was still worrying about what might be coming on other nights. I was right to be concerned.

On Sunday, the Mobe had planned to begin its actual demonstrations against the war and to protest the convention with marches and picketing around some of the hotels where delegates were staying. I helped organize a picket in front of the Conrad Hilton on Michigan Avenue, the major hotel for convention delegates. Later in the afternoon, a march of several hundred people from Lincoln Park—led by the effective co-leaders of the Mobe, Dave Dellinger, Rennie, and Tom—joined the picket lines. In the meantime, the Yippies were setting up in the park for a concert by the MC-5, the only band that showed up in Chicago. By late afternoon, the park had filled up with people, and there was music, balloons, and free food.

It didn't take very long before things became less idyllic. When the electric power for the band failed, there were minor clashes between small groups of police and young people, resulting in several protesters being clubbed and arrested. But things calmed down fairly quickly, and there were still a lot of questions about what people might do when the cops tried to enforce the curfew that night and how rough the cops might be. Before the 11:00 p.m. curfew, I was talking with a group of marshals, along with some others, when Tom and Wolfe were grabbed by two cops who had seen them deflating the tires on an unmarked police car. Tom had been under constant surveillance, and he and Wolfe were trying to give him a break from being watched by the police. Acting without any plan, and only reacting to what we saw going on, a group of us crowded around the cops and Tom and Wolfe, chanting to let them go. There were a lot of us, and only the two cops, so they released them.

At 11:00 p.m., the cops again moved to clear the park, only this time much more aggressively. With a few other marshals, I moved in front of their skirmish lines, encouraging people to leave and telling them there was no good place to fight where they were. But even though most people slowly gave way and moved west out of the park, some kids resisted, throwing bottles and lighting fires in trash cans. One of them was caught by two cops who clubbed him repeatedly in the head and left him bleeding on the ground. Once the police were at the border of the park, they didn't stop as they had the night before. This time they crossed over into the nearby neighborhood and began chasing and clubbing anyone they could—kids, local residents, newspaper reporters, and photographers—as they rampaged to clear the streets. There wasn't even the charade of arrests; it was all brutal, physical punishment for daring to be out on the streets.

I was still walking behind a small crowd of people I was helping to herd out of the park when in front of me, two cops used their clubs to beat a kid who was on his knees with his arms up, trying to deflect the blows. Then another cop caught me from behind and clubbed me hard on my upper left arm and back. But he was more interested in chasing down a group of three or four kids who were taunting him with cries of "Pig!" so I luckily managed to get out of the way and into a sheltering doorway. Small groups of cops were everywhere, hitting, jabbing with their clubs, and beating anyone they caught. Some of the protesters tried to fight back by throwing rocks or bottles, then running and turning back to scream at the cops, and then maybe throwing something else before running again. My arm was hurting and I'd had enough, so I got to my car and left. The hit-and-run fighting on the streets went on into the early hours of Monday morning.

On Monday afternoon, after an uneventful opening of the convention that no one on the streets was paying any attention to, the police arrested Tom and Wolfe in the park again for messing up the cop car the evening before. Rennie quickly organized a march downtown to demand Tom's freedom. After the previous night's violence, none of us were particularly happy about cooperating with the demands of the cops to stay on the sidewalk. The people marching were bunched closely together, loudly jeering the cops or chanting for Tom to be freed. The crowd also occasionally heckled the demonstration marshals for trying to keep folks moving and as separated from the cops as they could be. By the time we got just south of the Hilton on Michigan Avenue along Grant Park, people had had enough of being "permitted" to protest. Twenty or thirty young kids in the march broke away, ran up a gently rising slope to the statue of Civil War General Logan riding his horse, and climbed the statue. A few carried up and waved Vietcong flags. I stood at the bottom of the hill, behind a line of angry cops who circled the statue in preparation for winning it back. I was worried about kids being hurt, but I was also experiencing a fierce joy and pride at their defiance. The cops didn't wait long. They charged into the small crowd at the base of the statue, then struggled to grab and remove the two or three kids who had climbed to the top of the statue and seemed determined to resist them.

That defiance carried over into the park that night. I was walking around the park close to eleven, and I could hear people arguing in favor of getting out of the park before the cops attacked and back onto the streets where it would be easier to fight back. Some did leave, but there was a strong core that weren't going to exit the park. I watched them build a flimsy barricade by piling together park benches, picnic tables, and ripped-up wooden fencing they tossed over the trash baskets. The impossibly bright lights from TV camera crews trying to film what was going on would briefly illuminate the building of the barricade and other small slices of the park. In the background were loudspeaker warnings from the cops about the curfew. Each one drew chanted responses of "We won't go! We won't go!" When a police car moved slowly toward the barricade, protestors threw stones at it. When the car stopped, its windows were broken by a barrage of more stones. Other cops began lobbing tear gas canisters over the barricade. Some of them, outfitted with gasmasks, began assaulting anyone they could reach before the gas finally drove almost everyone out of the park.

I was gassed. My eyes wouldn't stop tearing up and they burned. I forced myself to take short, shallow breaths, but my chest still hurt. I kept trying to spit out the saliva collecting in my mouth. Walking out toward Old Town, I knew enough not to rub my eyes, and finally got some sort of liquid to rinse my face and eyes from one of the volunteer nurses who was working on the streets with the Medical Committee for Human Rights. The only cops I saw who were not using their clubs to viciously beat people either had shotguns and pistols out in a far more menacing posture, or were wearing the white shirts of police lieutenants and captains and were just watching the show. I avoided getting hit that night, but shotguns in the hands of enraged cops scared me, and when I drove home, I was unsure what I should be doing on the streets.

I spent most of Tuesday resting in Lincoln Park with lots of other people, thinking and worrying about what would come that night. I spoke to Jerry and we shared war stories—where we'd been, what we'd done so far. He was filled with energy and excitement. After a few minutes, he bounded off to introduce a new speaker named Bobby Seale, who was the Chairman of the Black Panther Party, an avowed socialist, disciplined revolutionary black political organization, which was deeply admired by the white Left. Nobody in the Yippie or Mobe leadership really knew Bobby; he was a last-minute substitute for Eldridge Cleaver, an even more prominent member of the Panthers who people did know. Bobby gave a tough speech to an enthusiastic crowd of young people about resisting the pigs and an oppressive, racist power system.

That evening, knowing the fighting would begin again in both the park and the streets, I couldn't bring myself to leave the park, even for the "Anti-Birthday Party" for LBJ that the Yippies and the Mobe were hosting at the Coliseum, an indoor space south of the Loop. I stayed in the park, and I was there to see a group of grown-ups, some wearing clerical collars and helped by a few of the kids, carry a big wooden cross into the park. They conducted a long prayer service I didn't pay attention to. I was certain it was intended to ask for peace, and possibly even understanding and forgiveness, but I wasn't ready to forgive anybody, and I was certain there'd be no peace that night.

There wasn't. On Tuesday night, with no particular provocation from the people in the park, but acting on the city's determination to clear the park and punish demonstrators, the cops threw more gas at us more quickly. They had borrowed a gas-dispensing machine of some sort from the army, rigged it onto a garbage truck, and then sent the truck into the park. But while the lines of gas-masked cops were able to catch and beat some people, we were all faster out of the park that night. On the streets it was all hit-and- run action, with small groups of protestors throwing rocks and bottles, running away, and then anxiously waiting for another cop car to come by to throw rocks at. I joined up with a small group on the street and did my own share of throwing rocks and bottles at police cars.

Whatever had been going on inside the convention, and whatever would happen, had become almost completely irrelevant to any of us. The convention was happening in a different, almost imaginary city. Reality was what we were experiencing on the streets.

Wednesday, August 28, was the only day a permit had been granted for a protest rally, and the Mobe was determined to make use of it. I went to a morning meeting in the Mobe office with many other marshals and heard the Mobe leadership decide that people would be given choices. After the rally at the Grant Park bandshell located just across from the Loop, they could join a nonviolent march to the Amphitheatre where the convention was being held, leave the park and gather in front of the Hilton hotel on Michigan Avenue for a rally, or just disperse and do what they could to stay safe.

More out of a continuing sense of obligation than any belief that it would make any positive difference, I joined in helping the marshals form a ragged protective line between the thousands of people at the bandstand rally and the more disciplined ranks of police who were lined up with their clubs on the west side of the crowd. I paid almost no attention to the speeches, even though I saw and heard Jerry early on. I was watching the cops, trying to anticipate any menace. Younger kids and the tougher veterans of the previous nights in the park were there as well. But I was also a little stunned at how many classic anti-war, older, straighter people were there, sitting in white folding chairs and on benches. It was almost as if they hadn't gotten the news that the demonstrations against the war in Chicago had become dangerous and violent.

While the speeches were still going on, some kid decided to climb the flagpole and lower the flag to half-mast as a signal of distress. When the cops suddenly charged into the crowd to get to him, they knocked me over and made sure I was well-trampled, then moved on without even bothering to hit me. They knocked over other marshals and people seated in chairs, randomly clubbing people in a rage and fury. As the incident escalated, Rennie ran over to try to help re-form the marshal line, but the cops recognized him, clubbed him to the ground, and continued beating him bloody until he managed to crawl away under some fencing. Rennie would later need thirteen stitches on his head.

Then the cops pulled back almost as quickly as they had charged, and the rally continued on with its speeches. Tom made an angry plea, demanding people join him on the streets, and then Dave gave people the option to join the nonviolent march he would lead to the Amphitheatre, to just stay in the park, or to join in "other actions." Acting out of my last shreds of obligation, I joined the other marshals who were helping people line up to march with Dave and other Mobe leaders out of the park.

Dave was at the head of the somewhat frightened but determined crowd. Despite his last-minute, heroic-sounding public declarations, nobody was seriously thinking anymore about actually getting to the Amphitheatre where the convention was being held. Instead, most of us were hoping to simply move toward Michigan Avenue and the Hilton hotel that was housing many of the convention delegates.

I was walking toward the front of the crowd and off to one side when Dave and the rest of us were stopped by a couple of police cars and National Guard jeeps. Some command police officers and two or three armed guardsmen blocked the street and sidewalks we were on. The jeeps had semi-coiled barbed wire strung in front them from each bumper up to the top of the hoods.

I listened and watched as Dave patiently endured being stopped before stubbornly insisting he was going to continue on in a peaceful but determined manner to Michigan Avenue and the Amphitheatre. In the meantime, people in the crowd had discovered that there were unblocked streets just to our north that also led out of the park and onto Michigan Avenue. The whole back half of crowd, and then most of the people behind Dave, began half-running, half-flowing out toward the north and around the blockaded street. But Dave stayed in his quiet confrontation with the police and guardsmen.

I finally left him and joined the crowd crossing over the Jackson Boulevard Bridge into the Loop. I slowly worked my way closer to the Hilton, occasionally bumping into people I knew from Lincoln Park. I also talked with a small group of marshals, still together and determined to stay on the street and fight back against the cops whatever might happen.

Around eight that evening, police lines were stretched across Balbo, blocking any further movement south, and along both sides of Michigan Avenue. Thousands and thousands of demonstrators massed near the Hilton in front of the stationary network TV cameras that had been mounted in front of the hotel all week to catch the delegates come and go.

I never heard what I assume was a pro forma, half-hearted order for the crowd to disperse before the police simply charged. This time they were using clubs, fists, knees, and mace on anyone they came close to in the crowd. People at the front and along the edges of the crowd were fighting back and throwing rocks, and it all became a fierce swirl of fighting and people being beaten to the ground, arrested, and dragged into paddy wagons while still being clubbed.

I was toward the front of the crowd on the east side of the street, closer to the park than the Hilton, when it began. I heard men and women screaming as they were being hurt by clubs or sprayed with mace, but the first police rush didn't reach me immediately. I was soon clubbed on my left arm and side, but people around me had already started running to get away, so I had time and space to avoid getting trapped by the charging cops. I succeeded in disengaging from the crush of yelling and fighting and, a little dazed, I walked a short distance north up Michigan Avenue to the wide steps of the Art Institute.

Sitting on the steps of the museum, I smoked a cigarette and watched the surging crowds on the street. For the first and only time in my life, I thought that maybe a revolution could actually happen in America. I still take time to remember August 28 every year and have a drink or two for who we all used to be. The fighting in the streets lasted for what seemed like hours, until most of the crowd had either been beaten and arrested or had finally scrambled away onto the side streets away from Michigan Avenue.

On Thursday, I mostly avoided the crowds and speeches further south in the park. Still exhausted and angry, I sat on a patch of grass on the Grant Park side of Michigan Avenue with a few of the marshals I had worked with in Lincoln Park earlier that week; one of them had been with me in the street for a time on Wednesday night. But I was dangerously indiscreet as we talked about the fighting the night before, about who controlled the streets, and about how we could take control. I told them how my car, with its tank of gasoline, a six-pack container of thin-glassed soda bottles in the back seat along with a pile of dirty clothes and a high phosphate laundry soap like Tide was all we needed to seriously contest the ownership of the streets.

Unfortunately, one of those marshals listening to me was an undercover cop.

After the convention ended, the demonstrators went home. By September, when I wandered back to Northwestern, I was more convinced than ever that figuring out how to turn people into professional revolutionaries was important work. What other lesson was one to take from the use of unrestrained police violence to prevent and punish people who were trying to exercise their free speech rights to protest a war?

I started pursuing my new goal by meeting with the head of the Salvation Army College for Officer's Training in Chicago to get permission to do participant observation at the school. I would hang around, ask a few questions, and talk with the students. But mostly I would simply watch what was happening and take lots of field notes. Most people think the Salvation Army only consists of the uniformed bell-ringing folks who collect donations during the holidays, or those who manage secondhand stores for clothes and furniture. But there is more to them. The uniforms are there for a reason. The Salvation Army has a distinctly militant history in England, and if you look a little more closely, you might see an ideologically motivated, disciplined, specially-trained, quasi-military cadre with a lifetime commitment to radically change the world. Their ideology was a version of evangelical Christianity, and the Army's self-proclaimed "soldiers of Christ" wanted society to better reflect Christian ideals. But in my mind, what their school was trying to accomplish didn't seem too different from the goals of the early cadre training of Chinese peasants in the Hunan hills during the Long March.

Through much of the fall and winter, I hung out at the Salvation Army College, went to seminars at Northwestern, and stayed in touch with political friends in New York. During this time I had no idea that my phone was tapped or that I was being followed by both local cops and federal agents.

Nixon was elected president in November. He defeated Hubert Humphrey, who had been nominated at the conclusion of the bitterly divided convention in August against the backdrop of news footage of the street battles between demonstrators and the Chicago police. The election was ultimately decided by people who were frightened or offended or angry about the war in Vietnam, the increasingly strident and conflict-ridden demonstrations against the war, the violence in the cities that followed King's assassination, the black revolutionaries carrying guns, and all the long hair and dope smoking and loud music they saw on TV. They didn't understand why the government couldn't just stop such things from ever happening, punish those who needed to be punished, and do whatever needed to be done to make it all stop.

Nixon said he would bring back law and order, and that he would offer new leadership to deal with the war. Just enough people, who lived in the right places, believed him. He won by less than 1 percent of the popular vote, about 500,000 out of 73 million votes cast. But his 301 electoral college votes far outweighed Humphrey's 191. George Wallace, the segregationist third-party candidate, won five states in the Deep South, 13 percent of the popular vote, and thirteen electoral college votes. None of it was what anybody on the left considered good news, but nobody was expecting anything good to come out of the election except for the possibility that it might give more people even stronger reasons and motivations to fight against the war.

When I visited New York, I speculated with friends about who might be indicted for the things that happened in Chicago. It now seemed almost certain that the newly elected Republicans would use the courts to hammer at the kinds of people they didn't like. Tom, Rennie, Abbie, and Jerry were on everybody's list; Dave was on most of them. People thought maybe some of the other Mobe leaders would be included. Some folks suggested the list would include the singer and political activist Phil Ochs, or more likely Stu Albert, Jerry's longtime friend and political comrade, who had his own solid and deserved reputation as a serious hard left activist with a comfortable Yippie style. How many people might be indicted? Which women might be included, we wondered. A few people seemed to want to be indicted. My name never came up.

There had been news reports that in the waning days of the Johnson administration, his attorney general, Ramsey Clarke, had refused Mayor Daley's demands to indict people who were responsible for the demonstrations and conflict on the streets of Chicago. But it was reported that John Mitchell, Nixon's former campaign manager and new attorney general, was actively and enthusiastically pursuing federal indictments against the anti-war demonstrators in Chicago. And his perspective on who should be indicted and what they should be indicted for was grounded in the harsh "law and order" promises of the new administration and a desire to quickly demonstrate that those promises were going to be kept.

Because we didn't really think of ourselves as individuals representing something, we overlooked the fact that other people could choose to see us that way. We didn't seriously consider that the new Republican administration might deliberately choose to indict a collection of people who they thought embodied all the anti-war activists and counterculture that enraged them. These people could be presented as representing all the threats and commotions that the broader public just wanted the government to take care of and to stop. And from that perspective, I was a reasonable enough candidate to represent all those "wild-haired students."

There was also a special provision in the 1968 Civil Rights Act, which was passed in the days immediately following King's assassination and primarily outlawed housing discrimination based on race, that the new Justice Department could use to go after us—the "Anti-Riot Act." It was also known as the "Rap Brown Law," named after the former head of SNCC who had been photographed and recorded giving a speech in

Cambridge, Maryland, in the summer of 1967. In the speech, H. Rap Brown had denounced white-dominated society and urged blacks to fight back, and later that same evening, there had been gunfire exchanges between local police and black residents. The state charges of inciting a riot against Brown were ultimately dropped, but some people believed the outbreaks of urban violence across the country in 1967 were caused by "outside agitators"—people like Brown who instigated violence in communities where they did not live. The Anti-Riot Act in the Civil Rights Bill was a sop to such thinking, and it gave the federal government an additional, more direct way to go after such people.

Using that provision of the law, the Republican administration's Justice Department ruined an otherwise lovely day in March 1969—just before spring happened—and dramatically changed my life forever. Months removed from the chaos of the previous summer, I was living a reasonably quiet life on the North Side of Chicago as a graduate student at Northwestern. That afternoon, when I returned home to the apartment I shared with my wife and very young son, I walked into the wailing of a calamity. Our son was on the living room floor happily watching TV, so whatever was going on didn't involve him. I tried to ask my normally stolid mother-in-law, who had been babysitting, what was wrong, but she seemed incapable of uttering any coherent words. All she could get out were a series of anguished, keening noises announcing a disaster. I tried to calm her down, but before she could gather herself enough to answer, the phone rang. On the other end of the line was Donald Janson, a reporter for the *New York Times*. He said he had already called once and hung up after my mother-in-law's near incomprehensible reply, but that he'd somehow figured out that I was on my way home.

Janson wanted to know if I had any comment about my being indicted, along with seven others, on federal charges of conspiracy to cross state lines to do terrible things during the Democratic National Convention in Chicago the year before. My first instinct was to not say anything until I knew more about what was going on, so I fumbled to find some sort of inane, uninteresting answer that wouldn't be useful to quote. When I hung up the phone and turned on the TV, I learned that my seven codefendants and I were each looking at the possibility of ten years in prison. Some specific charges against us were mentioned, and mine sounded pretty serious: teaching and demonstrating the use of incendiary devices to disrupt interstate traffic.

I knew practically everybody else who was indicted: Tom Hayden was one of the founders of the Students for a Democratic Society and a longtime leader in the anti-war movement. We had briefly first met years before when Jerry and I visited the SDS national headquarters in Chicago, and we had a little more contact during the Chicago demonstrations. I had initially met Rennie Davis, another early SDS leader, in 1966 when he was working in Chicago's Uptown area as a community organizer among poor white Appalachian immigrants before he became a full-time anti-war activist. I only knew Dave Dellinger, a lifelong pacifist and social justice campaigner who was utterly committed to nonviolent resistance, from our few times together in Mobe meetings or demonstrations during the August protests. The same was true for John Froines, a junior faculty member at a college in Oregon who was another SDS community organizer alumnus and who had been a marshal for the Mobe. But Jerry Rubin was one of my oldest friends. He had first become a leader in traditional anti-war demonstrations, and then a full participant in the Yippie political and cultural craziness along with Abbie Hoffman, who I had originally met through Jerry a couple of years before. I didn't know Bobby Seale, the chairman of the then notorious Black

Panther Party, at all, though I had heard his speech in Lincoln Park during the demonstrations.

Except for John and me, who were more or less foot soldiers in the political struggles against racism, poverty, and the war through the sixties, the other people indicted were people my father would have called "*machers*" in those fights. They were people who made things happen; important people, publicly prominent enough to be pretty well-known by much of the national media. The fact that there were no women and no people from the Latinx or LGBTQ community as part of our group was simply a measure of the times, and a measure of how stupid, biased, unknowing, and unprepared for the future the government was.

While I certainly wasn't thrilled by the news of my newfound legal troubles, I never felt frightened. My political commitments had directed the way I had led my life for almost ten years. And if those commitments led me now to a particularly difficult and dangerous place, it wasn't completely surprising. It was just something that had to be lived through. I wasn't being brave. It was more that I didn't think there were a lot of alternatives available (or really, any at all).

After the indictments, any notion that I could simply continue to be a graduate student who'd done a little political work and had an interesting collection of friends was quickly trashed. The media touted my membership in what was now being called the "Chicago Eight." And there was a lot of early media attention on the eight of us. Jerry and Abbie gloried in it. In one TV interview Jerry, Abbie, and Dave gave, Jerry happily claimed that he had received "the Academy Award of protest" while Dave hovered in the background, hoping the cameras would give airtime to his insistence that the anti-war movement would continue growing no matter what. Rennie, who had been living in Hyde Park, used the moment—with me at his side in a nonspeaking role—to threaten more protests in the streets against the war and in support of the "anti-war activists and leaders" who had been indicted.

Over the next several months, the public's response to the indictments was largely shaped, recorded, and magnified by the three television broadcasting networks that then dominated the dissemination of news and political discourse in the country. They devoted noticeable airtime to the government's charges against us, to the better-known defendants, to our upcoming trial, and to the continuing anti-war protests around the country. The daily newspapers in major cities, and influential weekly news and opinion publications with meaningful national readership, also devoted time, articles, and analysis to the indictments. The trial increasingly began to be viewed as an event with important consequences for the rights and possible limits of free speech and for the government's efforts to contain and limit anti-war activity. The alternate or "underground" press tried to reach beyond the audiences of traditional media to speak to younger people living on campuses or on the margins in cities like New York, Chicago, and San Francisco. With political screeds against the government, and lurid, vulgar, and funny political cartoons and images, they tried to rally the anti-war and counterculture communities to support the defendants.

An example of the rapidly emerging importance of the trial in the overall content and tone of national political news is contained in a densely written, two-page letter to the editor of the *New York Review of Books* in June 1969. That publication was then the unquestioned bastion of liberal, politically engaged, intellectual and cultural elites, who believed their analyses of power and their essays about what was deemed "relevant" literature in America would have positive and meaningful social impacts. The letter denounced the indictments as an "ominous challenge to political liberty" and claimed the Anti-Riot Act was subverting the First Amendment and could serve as the potential "foundation for a police state in America." The letter pleaded for financial support for the defendants and was signed by nineteen authors, academics, essayists, and artists, all of whom were certain to be well-recognized and respected by the readers of the *New York Review of Books*.

In the midst of the commotion and anticipation of the trial, I'd also met a couple of times with Irv Birnbaum, who had been designated as our local, pretrial attorney. Irv had years of experience in the local and federal courts in Chicago, often defending anti-war activists. He had a fairly harsh and gloomy notion of what the trial might be like for us all. Rennie and I also talked about how to approach the trial politically. He saw it as an important, new platform—almost a gift—from which the anti-war message could be even more strongly and broadly communicated. I simply accepted the fact that it was going to be a loud political trial, a fight that would conclude with us going to prison. I had read enough political history, and had participated long enough in our own country's recent political struggles to understand that a vindictive, punishing trial by the government was an almost expected consequence of our politics.

Chapter 4

A Quiet Defendant

L eading up to the trial, there were meetings with a small but growing collection of people who would form the nucleus of the staff we'd soon need, as well as with lawyers who wanted to help. And after participating in enough meetings, the reality of the impending trial overwhelmed everything else in my life. My friend Dottie Palombo gave up her job to take over and run the defense office—the "Conspiracy" office. I felt I needed to give as much of myself to the work as she had. I had to tell my wife and small child that unless I willingly threw myself totally into the nightmarish, ever-building swirl and fight, I'd drown, and so I had to leave for a while.

I didn't do it well, and I wasn't completely honest because I had already started a new relationship with Sharon Avery, a woman I had met in early staff meetings where we worked on organizing the office we would need during the trial. Sharon was in her early twenties and a graduate of Chicago's Art Institute. She had short blond hair and a preference for noticeably short skirts and tinted aviator glasses. I moved out of the apartment I shared with my wife and son, and by midsummer, Sharon and I were living together in her small studio apartment in Hyde Park, with its Murphy bed, acid orange sheets, and startlingly bright green pillow cases.

Despite frequent cross-country telephone calls and a few meetings between different clusters of defendants with and without lawyers, we didn't really have a defense strategy. The eight of us really were not a group, more just a collection of people who had been selected by government prosecutors to be on trial together. We didn't agree on much. While we were linked by a shared commitment to end the war and change America, we had landed on the same streets and in the same parks mostly by default. There weren't that many streets and parks to choose from that made any sense. And while we were able to agree on the lawyers who would represent us in court, that was the only significant decision we were able to make together before the trial began.

The trial would be noisy. It was all about the war in Vietnam, drugs, racism, violence on the streets of Chicago, music, politics, sex, revolution, undercover police agents, the First Amendment, wiretaps, and poetry. It was overseen by a nasty, mean-spirited, easily caricatured judge, whose favoritism for the government and prosecution would have been laughable if he hadn't had so much power over our lives. We openly mocked him, fighting and ignoring him day after day in his courtroom and in the press conferences and speeches we gave all over the country. The newspapers loved it. We were about as famous as you could be before the internet, Twitter, Facebook, and Instagram.

None of us had any illusions about what the trial was about. It wasn't about finding out who was right and who was wrong on the streets, and it wasn't about high-minded principles like protecting constitutional rights to free speech. We all understood that the trial was just a more complicated and time-consuming continuation of the state's organized use of power and violence against dissent that had been used in Chicago during the summer of 1968.

Long before that summer, we had all experienced the ways that the government used its authority, rules, laws, threats, and police to prevent our efforts to end racism, fight poverty, end the war, and establish a freer, more equitable America. We'd all been in jail. We'd all chosen to live in opposition to the dominant politics and values of our country. The trial was another battle in what had become a war between a government that was defending itself, its economic power, and its dominant, oppressive culture against the changes we all believed would lead to a different and better future. For us, the only question about the trial was how we could most effectively fight back.

On the morning of September 23, we were in the federal courthouse in the Loop off Jackson and Dearborn. We were all on the twenty-third floor in a large, two-story high, wood-paneled room under front-to-back, wall-to-wall fluorescent ceiling lights that created what Abbie described best as "a neon oven." Sitting around the defendants' table with our lawyers were the eight of us who had deliberately, in defiance and with snide humor directed at the government charges, branded ourselves "the Conspiracy." We announced it loudly, repeatedly inviting everyone to join us.

The four defendants with somewhat shorter hair—Tom Hayden, Rennie Davis, David Dellinger, and John Froines—had known each other for what seemed like forever, several from the very earliest years of the efforts by the Students for a Democratic Society to support civil rights and change America for the better. Tom, Rennie, and Dave had worked hard together against the war (all three had already visited North Vietnam). A little to one side of that trio, but close, was John Froines, who had worked with Tom in the early SDS community organizing efforts.

Tom Hayden looked just like who he was—a bit lanky, black Irish, and like someone who maybe had a future lurking out there where he'd become a little bit of a drinker. But in those days, he was hard-edged, intense, and always fully engaged with whatever he had personally decided was the serious work that needed to be done. I hadn't much cared for Tom when I briefly met him years before at the SDS national headquarters on Sixty-Third Street in Chicago. Tom grew up Catholic in a suburb outside of Detroit, and he had gone to the parish school run by Father Coughlin, the anti-Semitic radio priest. It seemed to me Tom still carried at least a hint of that past with him. Lots of people said I was wrong about him; on the other hand, I wasn't the only one who cringed at that small biographical detail. But more relevantly and worse in my opinion was Tom's certainty that he was right, that he knew what was best for other people. That certainty might cloud over for a bit sometimes. Its edges might soften due to stress, exhaustion, too many political alternatives to choose from, or honest desperation for some other kind of life, perhaps one with political work on a less grandiose scale and with more room for private joys. But it was still there.

I'll admit Tom had plenty of personal history that could support his belief in the correctness of his own judgments and vision. He was the primary author of the SDS's founding document and had worked in the South and as a community organizer in Newark. Ferociously intelligent, he had long been extraordinarily important in the anti-war movement and national demonstrations. He had been in personal contact with elite politicians, high-level *apparatchiks* of the Democratic Party, and swarms of writers from the better liberal newspapers. But I'd already grown weary (if not yet suspicious) of people who were always certain they were right, whatever political side they might be on.

Rennie Davis was of another type. He had light brown hair and was about Tom's size. But with his thick-framed black glasses and the fact that he looked a lot younger than the twenty-nine years he actually was, he seemed less hard-edged somehow. Rennie's best trick was to be pretty much in control of how he presented himself, and how other people would at least initially see him. That was true when he'd been an SDS leader, a community organizer in Chicago's Uptown community with rural white migrants, or a particularly intense anti-war activist who had personally seen and felt the horror being inflicted on the Vietnamese people. But he could also present himself as an almost grown-up terribly sincere member of the better class of people, who as a youngster had won a 4-H award for inventing a whistle that stopped chickens from clucking so farmers could identify the ones that wheezed with a dangerously contagious illness and needed to be culled. Rennie played the "trustworthy" card really well.

He almost always was ready to play the role of mediator when things threatened to become unglued, both in the meetings between defendants and lawyers, and earlier that past summer in the meetings leading up to the demonstrations. He was always reasonable, never yelling. He and Tom had a very close, mutually supportive relationship, with Rennie always providing the moderating voice, administrating, helping to make things actually happen. As he intended, I always found him easier to talk to than Tom.

Dave Dellinger was a stocky middle-aged man in his mid-fifties, balding, and forever wearing the same tweedy sport jacket, white shirt, and tie. He was by far the oldest member of the group. If you didn't know his history, you'd be forgiven if you thought he might be a pharmacist near retirement, or a lawyer with a small, not necessarily very successful private practice in a medium-sized city (perhaps in Ohio). But he had been a jailed conscientious objector during World War II, and had helped organize a successful prisoners' strike against racially segregated dining in the prison. In all the years since, he had never really stopped waging public, purposeful, and aggressive nonviolent resistance to injustice, especially against the war in Vietnam. Watching Dave during the Chicago demonstrations, I thought he was as interested in sainthood as he was in tactical victories, and therefore a dangerous man to follow into a politics that didn't much reward martyrdom. Nor should it, I thought then and now.

John Froines might have been something else during his earlier years in SDS, when he and his wife Ann had been engaged in the community organizing efforts among the poor in northern cities, but when I had met him in Chicago that past summer, and in meetings before the trial began, he seemed mostly a particularly earnest academic type. Mustached, soft, and (if I was crueler) maybe a little flabby, John was mostly a listening participant in meetings (as was I), and almost always, because of his earlier SDS days and friendships I suppose, deferential to Tom and Rennie (which I wasn't). John would readily accompany Tom whenever he traveled to meet with a potential defense witness who was respected in the world of straight politics and who we were trying to convince to appear at the trial. I would regularly misjudge the depth and strength of John's personal political commitments, but in that particular crowd of competitive egos—louder and far less deferential defendants—that was easy to do.

Then there were the odder, longer-haired Jews who had known each other for a bunch of years: Abbie Hoffman, Jerry Rubin, and me. We had smoked weed pretty regularly and had worked on college campuses, in the South, and as organizers on the streets in San Francisco, New York, and Chicago. And even though I looked the part, back then I was rarely able to soften the hard edges of my political identity enough to actually join in the fun with Abbie and Jerry and all the rest as part of the Yippie crew.

Both the indictment and the media came close to fusing Jerry and Abbie together. They had already been a highly visible, loud, and often outrageous tag team in building the Yippies. Yet Abbie took much more naturally to his role as the politically relevant maniac than Jerry, who was often more deliberate and always more intense. Those tendencies would only be amplified in the courtroom.

Bobby Seale was also sitting at the defendants' table. Bobby was slender with dark brown skin and round, not extravagant natural hair. He exuded a very different demeanor than the rest of us. "Haughty" wasn't the word. Maybe "serious" or "determined," but I kept coming back to "righteous" and "strong." With Huey Newton, he had cofounded the self-declared revolutionary Black Panther Party for Self-Defense in 1966 and had helped lead all of the Party's major initiatives, including armed citizen patrols that monitored police behavior in Oakland to reduce incidents of brutality in black neighborhoods; the Free Breakfast for School Children Program; and a demonstration in 1967 by the Black Panthers where they carried rifles and shotguns into the California state legislature to protest a proposed law that would outlaw citizens' rights to publicly carry weapons.

Bobby really didn't know any of us. He had flown into Chicago for an overnight stay that past August, given two short speeches, and then left after less than twenty-four hours. But that was long enough for him to be snapped up as the representative of the newer, hard-edged, militant, and threatening radical black political movement. Bobby spent most of his time in the courtroom taking notes and writing on yellow pads of paper, paying close attention. When the trial began, Jerry was briefly finishing up a sentence from a California arrest for an anti-war demonstration, and he spent a little time with Bobby while they both were being transported by marshals back and forth between Cook County Jail and the courtroom. He told me he was impressed by how solid and settled Bobby was, and about his occasional flashes of humor. In the courtroom, Bobby didn't exhibit any humor. No surprise. He'd been indicted on state murder charges in Connecticut. Our trial was extra credit for him, a grand but nightmarish prelude that he'd participate in each day before returning to jail every night. When we were done, he'd go on trial again on those state charges.

Then there were our lawyers. We had settled on them in an early summer meeting. The consensus formed quickly—nobody objected, nobody had anybody else they really, really pushed for. The lead attorney was Charles Garry. He was the primary attorney for Bobby and the Panthers. Partially in deference to them, and also out of respect for Garry's well-deserved reputation in politicized criminal trials, we listened to him in that meeting as he made his demands. He'd make all the decisions, and there would be no funny business in the court. In an almost off-handed way he also suggested that one of us might be an informer. Mostly we just nodded our heads and agreed with him. Garry never got to our courtroom, though. A sudden illness, requiring surgery, and the judge's unreasonable refusal to grant a brief, temporary delay to the beginning of the trial until Garry recovered meant that Bobby wouldn't have his own trusted attorney at his side. It also meant we wouldn't be constrained by what Garry thought our courtroom defense or behavior should look like.

One of the two lawyers who were with us was Lenny Weinglass. Lenny was in his late thirties, a gentle, warm man who evoked affection from the rest of us. He had met, worked with, and befriended Tom when Tom had been a community organizer in Newark. At the beginning of the trial, Lenny was already fairly convinced that we would have little chance of avoiding ten-year sentences. But he still had far more faith in the law than any of the defendants did. His intensity was partially cloaked by his graciousness, affability, and sincerity. He listened, and he always tried to understand and make sense of what we all talked to him about—all the details about what each of us had done, what each of us had thought back in the summer of 1968 and the months before. Then he would worry and try to figure out how those details might show up in the prosecution's case and what to do about them, or perhaps how we might present those details to the jury ourselves.

Lenny was good-looking in a slightly frazzled way, his hair was already too long not to be noticed, and we were his first federal trial. He was extraordinarily hardworking and ferociously committed to us and the trial. Night after night he'd be reviewing the daily trial transcripts, preparing cross-examinations, preparing our witnesses, and participating in sometimes raucous discussions with the defendants about trial strategy. As time went on, he almost always hid his despair at what the trial and the law itself had degenerated into during our months in that courtroom as a result of the judge's actions and decisions and the prosecutors and their claimed evidence.

Our other trial attorney was Bill Kunstler. Bill had worked in the civil rights movement in the South; he defended the Freedom Riders in 1961 and continued on from there. He knew lots of the people we knew. He was tall, lean, and more flamboyant than Lenny. In his early fifties, his hair was just beginning to grow a bit, and if he had tried harder, he might have been able to pretend fairly convincingly that he was the calm adult in the room. Of course he wasn't, and the pretense that he was wore pretty thin as the weeks of the trial turned into months. But in court Bill always had a quick manner, and his emotionally rich voice often had a dramatic flair when he questioned prosecution witnesses or other folks we put on the stand. He sometimes seemed to be performing a particularly enjoyable role in a grand movie that was playing out in his head. His occasional slight distancing from the details—his dedication to performance—would sometimes get in the way of how much attention the defendants gave to Bill's notions when we all met and argued over the course of the trial and the strategy we should pursue.

The judge overseeing the trial, Julius Hoffman, was small, old, crinkled, bald, and absurdly supportive of the prosecution. With a self-satisfied sneer, he openly relished and continually referred to his own power over the court. He was sarcastic, hostile, and demeaning toward our lawyers and us. When he became angry over a perceived coarseness, an over-persistence in questioning, an argument from one of our lawyers, or the quite real and intended insults from the defendants—which regularly happened day after day—his jaw would tighten, he'd lean forward in his large chair, and through clenched teeth he'd remind us all we would pay for "bad behavior" in his court.

City officials and a great many policemen, some in uniform and others who had worked undercover during the demonstrations, testified for the prosecution. Every morning in the bitter Chicago winter, there were long lines of people who supported us outside the federal building who hoped to get one of the limited spectator seats. Inside the courtroom, intimidating federal marshals watched over the few who were lucky enough to get in. There were reporters, authors, artists, Hollywood folks, and political activists of every sort. They came from Beverly Hills and the grand apartments of the Dakota in New York City, but they also came from the college towns and flyover country in between.

In 1969, the dissemination of political news was almost entirely concentrated in the hands of the three national TV networks with regular evening broadcasts, the newspapers based in a half-dozen or so major cities, and a relatively small collection of news and opinion magazines with broad national distribution. That media world covered our trial constantly. If we weren't the lead story, we were very often close to it, and drawings from the trial of witnesses and the defendants were regularly splashed across broadcast screens and news magazines.

During the trial I met and got to talk with lots of famous people. There was Benjamin Spock, who had written the famous baby books and who had earlier been indicted and tried by the federal government himself for conspiracy to aid draft resisters. Talking with us in one of the smaller rooms that we used for our meetings with lawyers and witnesses, he was particularly calm and unhurried. He seemed quite convinced everything would work out well and that the government would fail to convict us.

Jon Voight and Dustin Hoffman also visited the courtroom soon after *Midnight Cowboy* had opened. They deliberately sat in the back of the spectator section rather than on the front benches where the guests who had been specially invited by the defendants, prosecutors, or the judge would sit. They didn't want to possibly distract the jurors in case they were recognized. In our brief conversations with them, they were reticent in their opinions about how they thought the trial was going or how it might end, but they were entranced by our efforts to resist the government in the courtroom.

The artist Larry Rivers came for a couple of days, sitting in the front rows. He made an oversized pencil sketch of Artie and Malik Seale, Bobby's wife and young son. Sharon, the woman I'd been living with was sitting next to Larry, and when she excitedly handed the sketch to Artie, she explained how rare and potentially valuable it was. Artie just folded it up and stuffed it into the small bag she had with her, and Sharon almost cried as she saw the sketch reduced to worthless, crumpled, smudged paper.

Nicholas Ray, who had directed James Dean in *Rebel Without a Cause*, came to the trial often over a couple of weeks. He told us he was thinking of making a movie about it. And when Abbie, Jerry, and I followed up with him about Abbie's idea to have Groucho Marx testify at the trial about humor and satire, Nick got us Groucho's personal telephone number. With special joy I got to make the call, but Groucho expressed real regret about declining what he said would be "an honor." He laughed as he explained that he thought his last name might cause the judge to be biased against him and disregard anything he might say.

A defense witness or two dropped acid before they testified. Some folk and country singers (as one would expect) sang or tried to sing from the stand. And when a dark-haired, bushy and bearded, loving and lovely poet, Allen Ginsberg, had his testimony interrupted by the judge who agreed with the prosecutors' objections, he recited immortal and warning words from *Howl* to a judge who was full of pride and arrogance, and who could still easily use his power to jail us all.

Political calculation, argument, desire, and disappointment were always present among the defendants, our lawyers, the other lawyers giving us outside advice, and our staff members. The staff was vitally important; the complicated work of revolution and political trials never happens magically. It involves fundraising, bank accounts, staff stipends, office rent, apartment rents, opening and responding to a great deal of mail, handling contributions, contracting speaking engagements on college campuses, ground transportation, and airplane reservations. My old friend and comrade Dottie Palombo just took it all on. And with a ferociously committed, hardworking staff of young people, somehow it all got organized well enough so that everything almost always worked.

As for resolving the arguments and disagreements about the trial between the defendants, and between the defendants and the lawyers, far more often than not, we just agreed that we'd do it all. Whatever presentation or witness or legal strategy that was seriously proposed, we presented it in court at some point or another. And if those tactics made the trial a little longer than it otherwise might have been, or if we presented the jurors with different, possibly confusing versions of what might be important for them to understand in order to reach a favorable verdict, it wasn't a problem. Nobody really expected to win the jury over anyway. And none of us ever lost sight of the fact that we were in the middle of a vicious, deliberately oppressive political trial that was barely managing to masquerade as a criminal one.

Our task was to fight back, to present the reasons why we had acted as we did and why the government had acted as it did. We wanted to present political arguments to the jury, and more importantly, to the broader public, that would convince people to condemn the government, its war, and its efforts to crush dissent, social justice, and the emergence of a new, more open, kinder culture.

So we also were all involved in an endless series of speeches—they seemed to take place every other day—on college campuses and in city streets. And after the speeches, of course, clusters of young women would surround the stage, along with a smaller but distinct crowd of exceptionally good-looking young men standing behind them. All of them were hopeful for some sort of physical contact with the "Revolution" that had suddenly been made real to them in living, shouting, laughing flesh. And yes, there were often brief, quickly agreed upon encounters that were more appreciative or exciting gestures than they were romantic ones. There were a lot of drugs. The music was often good and almost always loud.

But in the midst of it all, while we were in that dreadful courtroom, each of us had to deal with the unexpected vast celebrity status that had been thrust upon us, and with the political storms that were still crashing different pieces of America against each other. We sometimes were able to manage a collective response to one political flash point or another, but sometimes we couldn't even agree on what an important political event was, much less agree on how we— "the Defendants"—should respond.

Stonewall was an example of something that didn't fit into most of the defendants' notions of an important political event. I disagreed. Stonewall was the Greenwich Village gay bar where, at the very end of June in 1969, a police raid had morphed into an insurrection. It was two nights of rioting by gays, transgender people, cross-dressing street prostitutes, and lesbians fighting back against the cops and against their own histories of oppression and public denigration. Stonewall would later be seen as one of the birthplaces of the gay liberation movement and the continuing, explicit, and unapologetic struggle for LGBTQ rights.

But that wasn't understood, and it was barely even dreamed about as summer drifted into fall in 1969. Around that time, before the trial got underway, I was asked by two gay friends to speak at a gay rights rally in Chicago they were helping to organize. Would I speak on the commonalities their struggle shared with the civil rights movement, about the linkages between their struggle and everything else that the counterculture, left politics, and the anti-war movement were all about? Of course I would. Where and when?

A few days later, while I was visiting at the large South Side apartment where Tom, Lenny, Bill, John, Ann, and some others were staying, I casually mentioned the rally in Chicago I'd soon be speaking at and Tom exploded. What I remember best is Tom's absolute certainty and his loud conviction that what "the gays" were trying to do was demeaning and trivializing to the Civil Rights Movement. How could I even think of participating in that?!

I thought Tom was being a bit of a narrow-minded jerk. Worse, he seemed to have no real sense, no feeling or appreciation for how the changes in the world that we all had worked so hard to achieve had already expanded the sense of power and possibility for all sorts of people, even though those changes were still incomplete. But those partially realized changes had already reached into different communities of people who had been pushed aside—people who were tired of hurting, tired of having their hurting ignored, and who were now ready to fight back.

This was especially true of people who were suffering because of hate and ignorance, because of the cruelties— enforced by the unequal distribution of social, political, and economic power in America—of everyday expectations about what their "place" in the world should be. To me, the brutality and oppression of the poor families that I had lived and worked with just a few years earlier smelled and felt an awful lot like the oppression the gay community was finally rising up against.

But it really was only 1969. Our trial would be starting soon, and there was the real possibility we all would be going to jail for ten years. I felt Tom's error in judgment was so profound, so warped by life as it used to be, that I didn't bother to spend a lot of time arguing with him. I finally just left the apartment after telling him that I thought he was terribly wrong and that I was surely going to speak at the rally, which I did.

To most people, the trial seemed to begin in the expected manner, with the selection of a jury and opening statements by the prosecution and defense attorneys. But they were wrong. The real beginning, and the event that determined the early content and tone of the trial, had happened two weeks earlier at a pretrial hearing where the judge refused to grant a postponement of the trial until Charles Garry had sufficiently recovered from his gallbladder surgery and could be in the courtroom. That decision effectively denied Bobby his own attorney, and it established the primary dynamic of the trial for as long as Bobby was with us in that courtroom.

From the very beginning of the trial, Bobby argued in court—both standing up before the judge and while he was seated at the defendants' table—that he was being unfairly deprived of his attorney of choice and that he lacked the legal representation that was guaranteed by the Constitution. It started on the second day of the trial. Bobby had spoken with Garry on the phone from jail the night before. He had prepared detailed notes on a yellow pad, and during a morning conference between the defendants and our lawyers, we had all talked about what he intended to do.

Almost as soon as the judge took his seat behind his tall, wooden bench, before anything could really get started in the courtroom, Bobby stood up and went to the lectern from which the lawyers usually spoke. I thought Bobby was pretty clear. If he couldn't have his lawyer of choice—he didn't want Kunstler or Weinglass—he instead wanted to defend himself. Then he quietly returned to his seat.

The chief prosecuting attorney stood up and quickly argued against that possibility. The judge went into one of his little hunched-up, patronizing, and sarcastic frenzies that would become all too familiar to us as the trial went on. He ultimately denied Bobby the right to defend himself.

The judge based his refusal—and his assertion that Bobby was represented by Kunstler—on an arcane formality regarding a signed document that allowed Kunstler to briefly see an isolated Bobby in jail after Bobby had first been transported by federal marshals to Chicago from the west coast and had been unreachable by anybody for days. And that would become a continually repeated public clash in the courtroom. Bobby would insist he was without the lawyer of his choice, that he wanted to defend himself and cross-examine witnesses when they mentioned him in their testimony. The judge would then angrily "admonish" Bobby, ordering him to stop interrupting the trial and that he had Kunstler as his attorney. Bobby in turn would denounce the judge as a racist for denying him his constitutional rights. That would send the judge into a barely restrained, teeth-clenched fury. He warned Bobby of contemptuous behavior over and over again, and Bobby simply continued his brave and persistent demands in the face of injustice and threat.

While that struggle dominated much of the early energy and focus of the trial, in the second week some testimony by David Stahl—the deputy mayor who had negotiated with both the Mobe and the Yippies about demonstration permits—led to something that wasn't much noted at the time, but that made the stakes we were playing for chillingly real to me. Stahl's actual testimony that particular day caused a good deal of laughter around the defendants' table and mocking disbelief among many of the reporters in the courtroom. He claimed with a straight face that he had certainly taken it seriously when, during a meeting with the Yippies, Abbie "offered" that he and the Yippies would call the whole thing off and leave Chicago for $100,000 in cash. Many trial accounts that were written later at least noted Stahl's testimony, usually to point out the absurdity of what the prosecution was asserting. But what struck me in the heart happened in a press conference with Abbie afterwards. It was captured on film but not mentioned much in reports about the trial.

I was in the back of the room, watching in admiration as Abbie was being his quick, charming, amusing best self as reporters repeatedly asked him whether the story was true. He laughed. He said for sure he would have taken the $100,000, but as to whether he would have called the whole thing off, he just smiled slyly and shrugged his shoulders in an exaggerated way. A particularly aggressive and totally unamused reporter kept repeating in slightly different ways the same questions: "Would you have done it? Would you have taken the money?" "How much money would it have taken to have you leave—a million dollars?" and finally, "What was your price? How much is it worth to you?" And then Abbie, still looking amused and still smiling, asked back, "What's my price?" Then he added, "For the revolution?" And then, with the very slightest narrowing of his eyes, he answered slowly and calmly, "My life."

And I knew it was true. The trial had barely begun, and we were still able to laugh at what we saw as the government's brutish determination and dangerous (though clumsy) efforts to paint us all as supremely evil characters. But Abbie's simple statement, said with a smile I suddenly recognized as regretful and accepting, cut through all the personal defenses that the busy work of the trial and my emerging celebrity had provided me. It was my life, the lives of all of us that were at stake in our confrontation with state power in that courtroom. It wasn't likely I'd ever be able to go back and be who I used to be, and I might not even get the chance to try to become who I might want to be. It made me a bit sad, but I was also more determined than ever to be strong and see it all through no matter where it went.

The much more public fight in the courtroom between Bobby and the judge kept going on for more than a month. During that time, the government was using testimony from city officials and police officers to build its case against us. But the real struggle in the court wasn't between their version of what happened in 1968 in the streets of Chicago and ours; it was between the judge and Bobby's determination to secure his constitutional rights.

In the meantime, some of Tom's newer and younger SDS friends were planning what they hoped would be major anti-war and anti-government demonstrations in Chicago toward the end of the first week in October. Unlike the Stonewall riots, none of us had any trouble at all recognizing these demonstrations as a political event. The Weathermen, who had emerged that summer after an ideological split between different factions in SDS, were calling it the "Days of Rage." The idea was to run wild in the streets of Chicago to "bring the war home." They were preparing for violent confrontations with the police by equipping themselves with clubs, rocks, long sticks, helmets, and Vaseline on their faces to guard against mace. Many of the men wore reinforced cups and jock straps for further protection in the fighting they were sure would come.

None of the defendants suggested we somehow act together as a group in response to this particular piece of impending political theater. In this instance, every defendant was on their own, figuring out a way to deal with it or gracefully ignore it, though of course we all still wanted to maintain our credibility and our very public leftist political reputations.

For Dave it was the easiest of calls. His whole life had been defined by his commitment to nonviolent resistance to injustice and corrupt state power. He would remain opposed to any politics that called for and glorified violence, no matter what its hopes and goals might be.

Bobby, still locked away in jail every night, was able to participate in brief defendant-lawyer conferences that sometimes took place before or after we were in court. He shared the same opinion of the planned Weathermen action as Fred Hampton, the broad shouldered, charismatic, and smart young leader of the local Black Panther Party chapter. Fred was Bobby's trusted link to the Panthers and the political world outside of his jail cell and the trial. Fred called the planned demonstrations "Custerist"—a deliberately ignorant, foolhardy (if daring) adventure that was sure to end badly. I thought "Custerist" would probably prove to be an accurate description of the demonstrations.

Still, I quietly showed up in the park on the Wednesday evening of October 8, deliberately staying on the crowd's outer edges and acting more like an interested tourist than an intended participant. I saw Abbie also off to the side, and I hoped he was as ready as I was to bolt for safety if or when things got ugly. John was there, but I don't remember seeing Jerry or Rennie. Tom spoke very briefly and reluctantly to the couple of hundred people who were milling around, waiting for the action to begin. Even then I recognized that Tom's speaking didn't reflect his usual sense of certainty. Like the rest of us who were sort of there but not really there, Tom's agreement to speak wasn't even some sort of half-assed effort at maintaining his public reputation and legitimacy on the political left. It was more the fact that they had asked him to speak, and how could he deny an invitation to support—no matter how marginally—a left wing politics that had been so central to his life for so very many years? After all, the people gathered in that park were the tattered remnants of Tom's beloved SDS.

Despite everything we knew, and everything we had seen and done and were now living through in that courtroom, we all still had at least a cherished memory of a hope that America could learn and understand what was wrong and then change for the better. It was very hard, and sometimes impossible, to reconcile those nearly abandoned hopes in the face of an increasingly repressive government. But we were who we were. We had grown up and had begun to act politically in a very different country, even if it was only ten years before. And how we could incorporate and act effectively within the changing politics and tactics on the left that was now emerging was very much an open question for all of us.

That was the question laid bare in the park by Tom's half-mumbled words and the obvious increasing emotional and political distances between us and that small Weathermen crowd, an aspiring, fantasized, revolutionary hoodlum vanguard.

Almost immediately after the violence of the Days of Rage, and with far less personal drama for the defendants, the Moratorium to End the War in Vietnam occurred in mid-October. It was something all of us—along with nearly everybody else in the country—had no trouble recognizing as a political event, and one that we needed to, wanted to, and could fairly easily respond to as "the Defendants." The Moratorium was organized by several senior staffers from the former McCarthy presidential campaign. It had the broadest, most inclusive (or deliberately vague) goal to just "give peace a chance." Consequently, it was a nonthreatening, safe way for millions of Americans to gather together in cities and towns across the country to express their discontent with the continuation of the war. On October 15, in support of the Moratorium, we all wore black armbands into court. Before the day's official proceedings began, we draped American and Viet Cong flags across the large defense table, and Dave started to read aloud the names of American and Vietnamese war dead. Not surprisingly, when the judge and prosecutors showed up in the courtroom, they raged and shouted demands to remove the flags and have Dave stop his reading. At the lunchtime break, in the plaza in front of the federal building, Dave, Rennie, and Tom spoke to an enormous crowd.

There were a lot of demonstrations. They weren't only around the federal building in Chicago or on special days like the Moratorium, and they weren't just passive demonstrations with planned speakers. There were loud, raucous campus rallies and marches on the streets. There were bombings and bank robberies and campus ROTC buildings that burned. Far more enduringly, there were also the women's movement and gay liberation. Similar to the way the Vietnam War had overtaken and displaced much of the work by the New Left in the sixties for economic, racial, and social justice, a mounting anger was overtaking everything we thought we knew about political activism. It was a flat-out refusal by all sorts of people to willingly submit to external, illegitimated power anymore.

But in some weird ways, the trial was a protective shield for us as well. We could mostly manage by just acknowledging the changes without having to actually deal with them very much in our day-to-day lives. We had near full-time jobs as defendants. And we were stars. So we managed to stumble somewhat successfully around the evolving politics of the world beyond the trial. And at least we didn't fall down in public in ways that most people noticed.

Near the end of October, the judge began to more stridently emphasize that he would do something to stop Bobby's actions during the trial. And one day, after the jury had been excused for the afternoon, the judge explicitly warned Bobby that he could be bound and gagged so he could be present at the trial but no longer disruptive. Although none of the other defendants mention it in their own recollections of that hard time, in either the evening right before or after the judge's explicit warning, we all got together for a very tough meeting. With our lawyers, we talked with Fred Hampton and another Black Panther Party member, who insisted on Bobby's request and the Panthers' demand that we not intervene in any way with what Bobby would say or do, and with whatever would happen as a result in the courtroom. We agreed. We were committed to supporting Bobby in the way he wanted to be supported. We weren't happy about it, but as all of our personal histories might suggest, we took our political commitments seriously.

On the morning of October 29, the number of marshals in the courtroom had visibly increased. They now lined the three walls around the spectators' sitting area and the wall closest to the defendants' table. Bobby again demanded the right to cross-examine a prosecution witness who had mentioned him the day before, and the judge again warned what would happen if Bobby didn't stop his "outbursts." Bobby pointed to the large portraits of Washington and another founding father on the wall behind the judge and asked what could happen to him that would be worse than what had happened to the slaves those men had owned.

The judge reddened and ordered the marshals to take Bobby away and "deal with him." When several marshals started dragging Bobby out of his chair and toward the door next to the defendant's table that led to the holding cells, all of us jumped up around the table, trying to somehow get in the way of what was happening. But remembering the commitments we had made, we were constrained and ineffective, reduced to quietly cursing. The judge then called for a lunch recess.

When we got back, Bobby was carried out of the holding cell area and put down in a tall chair on the side of the defense table. His wrists and ankles were chained and strapped to the arms and legs of the chair. A multi-layered white cloth had been wrapped several times around his mouth and over his head. He was breathing hard through the cloth gag. Despite that early, preparatory meeting with Fred Hampton and our own attorneys' even earlier warnings of what might likely happen, we were still not prepared for the reality of it, and we were initially overwhelmed by the brutality of arbitrary judicial power. The judge, however, simply ordered the cross-examination of the witness on the stand to resume, as if it was just another afternoon in court.

The lead prosecuting attorney—with what was almost certainly a preplanned effort to respond to and soften the visual outrage of a strong, free black man in chains—stood up and proposed that if Bobby would be willing to be quiet, the judge should consider undoing the chains and gag. The judge, using the gentlest voice we'd ever heard from him, asked Bobby for an assurance—simply by raising his head up and down—that he would stop disrupting the trial. Instead, with his compelling voice only slightly muffled by the gag, Bobby again demanded that he had constitutional rights, including a right to speak. The judge quickly told the marshals that they hadn't done their job well enough and that they needed to do better. He called another recess while the marshals tightened and strengthened the gag. After a bit of time, the trial restarted again with Bobby still chained and more securely gagged. It was almost an impossible thing for the rest of us to tolerate, to do nothing about, but we had made the commitment.

The morning of October 30, we arrived in court to find Bobby even more tightly strapped into a chair. The other seven of us, with a combined history of so many years of radical activism and fighting racism and injustice in the streets, were quiet. Trying to be politically disciplined, we held on to the edge of the table or made fists so tight our nails dug into our palms.

But the federal marshals weren't very good a tying knots. Bobby's gag kept slipping and he kept trying to shout about his rights from behind the loosened gag. As he visibly struggled, the judge told the marshals to adjust the straps and gag. In their attempt, several of them ran to Bobby and accidently overturned his chair. Bobby said something through the gag like, "You're kneeing me in the balls." Despite our promises not to intervene, that was the ball game for all of us.

I'd been sitting at the back end of the table. Bobby was sitting around the corner to my right, with one or two defendants sitting between Bobby and me. We jumped up together and began grabbing and punching at the marshals crowded around Bobby. It only lasted for a minute or two. I ended up way too close to being on the floor under a large marshal. And then it was all over as if it had never happened. Everybody got up, returned to wherever they were supposed to be, and the judge called for a brief recess.

Like everybody else, at the conclusion of the trial I was given jail time for contempt of court for, among other things, shouting out the correct pronunciation of my name whenever some cop on the witness stand mispronounced it. But about that actual physical tussle with the marshals? Not another word.

Though it seemed obvious that things couldn't continue in the way they had, there was another day of court where Bobby was tied and semi-successfully gagged. Then, starting on the Monday of the next week, Bobby was unexpectedly in a regular chair, not bound and gagged, and sitting around the defense table with the rest of us. He was still declaring his rights to defend himself and cross-examine witnesses against him, and it was almost as if the chaining and gagging hadn't really happened. But just as our attorneys had predicted it would almost certainly end, the struggle between Bobby and the judge was brought to a public conclusion on that Wednesday. The judge declared a mistrial in Bobby's case, severed him from the trial, and sentenced him to more than four years in jail for sixteen different acts of criminal contempt in the courtroom. Without Bobby, we were no longer the Conspiracy Eight, and the media took to calling us the Chicago Seven. The name stuck.

For days afterward, the courtroom, as well as our meetings together with the lawyers, felt hollowed out. But the government made sure that the trial continued to grind on. With greater determination, we kept up our efforts outside of the courtroom to rally people to our cause and against the government's trial and its war in Vietnam. That work included press conferences on many afternoons during the trial's lunch breaks; we used a space set aside for us in the federal building. One of us would be seated at a long table in front of the microphones, and the rest of us would stand behind, looking terribly intent and supportive. There were always lots of TV and radio people recording it all.

I refused to speak at that table in front of the press. I foolishly hoped that I could minimize my own celebrity, and, if the trial worked out better than I thought it would, I could then quietly slip back almost unnoticed into radical political work that would be less glamorous but still meaningful to me. But in front of the audiences that gathered on college campuses, I joyously wallowed in my notoriety. All seven of us were speaking all over the country. Up on some stage I'd teach and shout against both the war and the trial, joking and threatening evildoers. I spoke from the heart about poverty and America and the revolution. Of course I also gloried in how pretty I was, and the stories I told were enchanting enough that the new friends I made often caused me to almost miss my plane back to Chicago for the trial the next morning.

I don't remember what college or university it was—maybe St. Louis, or perhaps somewhere in Ohio—but at the last minute, the school's administration decided to withdraw permission to use the campus building that had been set up for my speech. That decision provided an unintended but very real gift, ensuring maximum attendance and crowd rowdiness. The students had quickly rented (or perhaps successfully browbeaten the owner into renting) a local movie theatre for the speech, and that night there was a particularly packed, boisterous, loud, and fun crowd. At the end, when the audience streamed out, loudly chanting slogans about ending the trial, freeing us, and ending support for the war, they headed to the campus ROTC building with what I suspected were not the clearest or best intentions. The two guys who were responsible for getting me to my flight and out of town decided that I'd probably be better off getting to the airport a little early, smoking a little dope, and talking to a few of their friends for a while instead of joining the rest of the crowd. I didn't disagree.

Another, perhaps better example of how our celebrity worked in real life was an evening Abbie and I spoke together at the University of Illinois at Urbana-Champaign. It was in an auditorium in front of a very large group of students. Abbie and I just took repeated turns telling stories. Some were funny, some dramatic. We demanded and pleaded for the audience's help to end the war and fight the demon government. We smoked a little weed as we talked while pretending we were only pretending to smoke a little weed. There was a lot of laughter and the bouncing energy and joy of the coming revolution. We asked for their money to help support our work in the trial, and people collected dollar bills and coins from the audience in big brown paper bags and then passed them to us up on the stage.

It was hard to keep track of those bags of money as both Abbie and I stopped for a little private time with different, particularly intense and supportive audience members. But somebody eventually dragged us away, bags of money in tow, into a running car so we could get to the airport and board the little private plane that would take us back to Chicago. We sat on the floor in the back of the plane, smoking more weed and counting up the money. The pilot had his little side window open and begged us to stop smoking because he was beginning to feel high himself.

Who, us? Why would two of the stars stop smoking?! We didn't pay any attention to him until the plane took an unexpected quick, slanting downward turn and all the coins and dollar bills we'd counted and neatly stacked up scattered like rain against the sides of the airplane. After he had straightened out the plane, the pilot went truly nuts, loudly and insistently demanding to know whether the money had made any holes in the aircraft. Abbie and I couldn't stop laughing as we kept asking each other what kind of hole the money would have made if it had all still been together in those big paper bags.

The trial continued to drone on. By the time the prosecution got around to making their case against me, it came as no surprise that their witnesses were all undercover and uniformed cops, and that they used a side helping of photos as evidence. But in the moment after they declared they were going to present evidence against me, there was also a preliminary, almost unnoticed moment that turned out to be an unexpected, but fairly clear twentieth-century life lesson about privacy in the twenty-first century.

The FBI agent who was always sitting at the prosecutors' table had left the courtroom. When he returned, he wheeled in a metal cart with two shelves—the kind that elementary schools used to use to schlep movie projectors and film reels between classes. On both shelves were piles and piles of paper transcripts from their taps on my home phone. Every political friend I had often joked about phone taps, but we seldom paid serious attention to the possibility they might actually be used on us. Occasionally, thinking about a tap, you might go outside to use a public phone, but how often would you do that just to talk with a friend? But in that courtroom, I remember thinking that privacy was definitely not something to ever assume or expect; you might be able to make special efforts and carve out some safe space, but it likely wouldn't be a lot of space and it wouldn't be private for very long. And that's surely truer now than ever before.

The government's case against me was basically that I was a dangerous person who they had known about for a long time. Lenny Weinglass had mostly been countering that notion in his cross-examinations by referencing my history of social work with kids and my work as a community organizer—all nonviolent and pure as a light snowfall in early winter. I'd been a peace-loving, caring person for years. Of course I was sitting at the table looking like a complete maniac, with wildly long black curly hair and a very full beard. If I was on an elevator and it stopped to let you on, I'd have completely understood if you decided you'd rather wait for the next one. That's why Lenny had me sitting so I was facing away from the jury.

The prosecution then wanted to enter into evidence a collection of photos that had been taken of me during the demonstrations. They had to let us see them before they could give them to the jury. As Lenny started looking through them, I heard him mumble under his breath something like, "Well, there goes that argument." He was talking about my image as a nonviolent and caring person. One disturbing photo showed me on an unscheduled march—out of Lincoln Park and over one of the bridges across the Chicago River towards the Loop and police headquarters—to protest Tom Hayden's arrest for having disabled an unmarked police car by deflating its tires. I was one of the more visible demonstration "marshals." We all wore black bandanas around our heads, and I had already begun growing a beard (though both my hair and beard were still pretty short). A news photographer had been getting in the way of the flow of the march and we were trying hard to keep people on the sidewalks to minimize immediate trouble with the police. So I charged the photographer with raised fists and a clearly threatening expression to move him out of the way. And just before I could get to him, he snapped the photo that was about to be presented to the jury.

Sitting in the courtroom, I agreed with Lenny that the photo didn't seem to demonstrate my lifelong commitment to nonviolence. So I slipped the photo out of the pile and placed it between the pages of a book I was reading at the defense table, then handed the rest of the photos back to Lenny. That was the pile of photos the jury saw. The lesson there I suppose is that in any political fight, you have to be ready and willing to take advantage of any unexpected opportunities that might improve your chances of winning.

Over the next few months, there was a continuing, seemingly endless stream of testimony from uniformed and undercover police and from paid informers. But it finally became time for us to make our own case to the jury. Practically everybody had a slightly different notion of the kind of defense we should mount. As the other defendants have noted in their own recollections of the trial, I was the least engaged person in our discussions of defense strategies. And there was reason for that. I had spent a lot of time in the courtroom reading—everything from *On War* by von Clausewitz and Sun Tzu's *The Art of War* to the *Tao Te Ching* by Lao Tzu and the *I Ching*. Part of that was because, in my head, I was often bouncing between different futures I might have to deal with—participation in more organized fighting in the streets and armed struggle, or being alone in prison for years. And I wanted to survive whatever came my way. Part of my reading was a simple distraction from the repetitive, boring, yet dangerous stories the government was weaving. And part of it helped distance and insulate me from the sense of threat and menace that pervaded the trial every day.

While I was reading, I was also watching the individual jury members as they listened to the prosecution testimony. They had been sequestered very early in the trial, and they were all living together in a fancy hotel in the Loop with marshals watching over them. From their reactions I could see, I thought that most of the jury was more than ready to accept as fact that we were bad people who should be punished in some way. If an individual juror occasionally appeared more skeptical of what they were hearing, I didn't believe there was really any way of knowing what we could say or present in court that might convince them to hold out and force a hung jury and a mistrial. So it was hard for me to stay involved in discussions about trial strategy that sometimes seemed driven by one or another defendant's ego or by a certainty I didn't understand or share.

We resolved our differences about trial strategies by simply deciding that we would present all of the defenses we thought were important. I was completely comfortable with that. And the others were mostly fine with the compromise because it still meant their favored strategy was going to be included. In my mind, since we didn't know which defense approach might work to support a juror's thinking that we weren't guilty, trying any strategy we could manage couldn't hurt, and it might even end up helping. Initially, Lenny and Bill (and many other outside lawyers who were advising us) might have preferred to present the jury with a more coherent and less complicated defense story. But we had taken control of things pretty much from the beginning of the trial and there was no going back. Instead, as Bill and Lenny would both later say, our trial taught them to work collectively with the defendants, and that was something they felt should be true in all political trials. One of the side benefits of a lengthy defense, as Tom later pointed out, was that it provided us with more time to speak on college campuses, increase public support, and prime the nationwide demonstrations that he believed would be the only thing that could reduce our jail time when we were convicted.

Our defense strategies included using tidy, standard-court-like factual presentations with witnesses and documents for the jury to examine; calling witnesses to provide alternative interpretations of things a prosecution witness claimed to have seen or heard; educating the jury about the war in Vietnam and its impacts on the people of Vietnam and here at home; raising arguments about how the First Amendment protected our intentions and acts; explaining what and why we did the things we did and challenging the notion of who really caused the violence in Chicago that summer; making a sustained effort to describe and legitimate different sorts of political dissent; making rollicking offers of what the counterculture looked and sounded like; making individual statements from the defendants' table about our disagreements with particularly flagrant mischaracterizations or lies about what we said and did, or why we did such things; deliberately disrupting the courtroom to highlight the political nature of the trial and mock the judge and show how the law was being illegitimately used; and including personal stories in formal testimony from a couple of defendants to show who we were and what we believed.

It was a lot. Maybe Tom or Lenny, on a particularly bad evening after a drink or two, might have actually created a list of all the different defenses we were going to try. But if they or anybody else made such a list I don't remember seeing it. And if I had, I don't know whether I would have laughed a lot or gotten a little sad. It probably would have depended on whether I was smoking weed or drinking, and what the day in court had been like just before I saw the list.

None of us expected to win over the jury. The optimistic ones among us occasionally hoped that we could win over at least one juror and then strengthen his or her resolve to stand against the others and that we'd end up with a hung jury. We sometimes talked about winning over public opinion—through media coverage of the trial and our appearances on campuses—and that somehow there would be massive demonstrations that could make a difference in how long we'd stay in jail. I'm not sure anyone ever got wrecked enough on drugs to actually fantasize that people would storm the Bastille for us, but maybe other people were doing weirder drugs than I was.

The defendants' direct testimony to the jury was given by Abbie and Rennie. We agreed the two of them could represent and speak for all of us and the two dominant streams of our politics: the emerging counterculture and the anti-war movement. Each of them was on the stand for a week.

Abbie didn't wait long to begin his assault on conventional court proprieties and traditional notions of self and politics.

When he was initially asked to give his name and residence, he rejected the idea that "Hoffman" was his last name. Instead, he favored what he thought would have been his grandfather's original Russian name, before "Hoffman" was attached as a "slave name" that was assigned after he had fled to America from Russian anti-Semitism. Abbie declared himself a resident of the "Woodstock Nation," which was a "state of mind" rather than a particular physical place. It went on from there.

Rennie talked about his traditional American upbringing, including his 4-H achievements, and identified his work to end the war in Vietnam as his primary occupation. During his testimony, he showed the jury a green, tennis-ball-sized metal object. It was a bomblet dropped by an American warplane over Vietnam, and he described how its explosive discharge of 300 steel pellets would affect living things—everything from a water buffalo to a child. There was more, including his account of what had happened when he was caught and beaten by police officers when they moved against the crowd in Grant Park the afternoon of August 28.

It was two weeks of testimony, cross-examination, and then Lenny's additional questions about issues that had been raised during cross-examination and that we believed might be used to more strongly make our case to the jury. We presented all of it in a context overwhelmingly controlled by a hostile, mean-spirited judge. Maybe it helped convince a couple of jurors that we were human, that we might not be quite as evil as the prosecutors painted us. Maybe it didn't.

When we were done, the prosecution presented its rebuttal case with more police witnesses. The winter days simply ran into one another without pause or any clearly defined beginning or end points. Still, our bedraggled supporters were lining up early in the bitter Chicago morning cold, hoping to be allowed into the courtroom as spectators.

As the trial droned on, it became clear that slow moving, relentless government repression doesn't really hide its face. Instead, it works to make all that threat and power that is mobilized against you a normal, everyday expected thing. It becomes something you can't avoid: federal marshals everywhere throughout your day; evening meetings between defendants and lawyers that are always about the trial and what the government might try next; outrageous claims against you and your friends that state functionaries and paid police informants regularly and easily make with the straightest of faces.

Those outrageous claims are dangerous because who knows what the jury believes and who they will trust? At the same time, the government required telegram notices to the marshals' office every time we wanted to travel out of town to give a speech. Every morning, we had to make sure we were in the courtroom on time. Listening to the judge belittle our lawyers and their arguments didn't produce fear, but instead threw a dulling, pervasive fog over us all. Implicit in it all was the argument that it was foolish not to submit to the reality of government power over your life.

It was something we refused to do. So we fought back. We fought back in the courtroom playing by their rules and by using nobody's rules but our own. And we fought back in press conferences and in speeches around the country. But sometimes—and almost always at a time and place the government alone chooses—their power and threat can be sudden and bloody.

In very early December, we were brutally reminded of just how high the stakes were in our battle against a government that was determined to use whatever power and force it had available to intimidate, punish, and destroy its enemies. On December 4, police officers assigned to the Cook County state's attorney conducted a predawn raid on an apartment occupied by Fred Hampton and other Black Panther Party members. With little or no warning, over eighty shots were fired into the apartment, killing Fred while he was in his bed. Mark Clark, a local Panther leader from Peoria, was also killed.

We naturally responded with public outrage, condemnations at press conferences, and loud speeches at rallies. But independent of all that, my sister Rayna, who had been coming to court off and on through the whole trial in a quiet, unobtrusive show of support, knew how devastated I was about the killings, and she responded to them in a quieter, more personal way. The morning after Fred's death, she came to court to give me a consoling box of Frango Mints—dark chocolate candy. They were a specialty of Marshall Fields, the grand department store on State Street in the Loop, and one of our favorite treats as teenagers. The marshals all knew Rayna was my sister, and on most days, just like our staff members and other special guests, she always got a seat on the spectator benches. But not that day. Instead, she was prevented from coming in and badly hassled about the small box of candy she was carrying. Two marshals grabbed her in the hallway in front of the courtroom and began hustling her away to who knows where. Fortunately, Sharon was on her way in to court at that same time. She saw it all happening and didn't hesitate to intervene loudly and effectively. I never got the candy, but Rayna escaped whatever fate those marshals had in mind for her.

I had my own private response to the police assault and murders as well. It seemed to me then that my response was completely reasonable, fully justified, and even a smart and necessary thing to do. I now think, however, that my response more sharply reflects the personal consequences of living under constant government threat and assumed surveillance than any words I might say about it. For me, the long accumulating stress of the trial, the isolation, and now the undeniably increased danger resulted in a sharply growing anger and desperation, an utter, eruptive refusal to passively submit to the possibility of state terror.

Sharon and I were living in her Hyde Park studio apartment. Most of the others associated with the trial— defendants, lawyers, and staff—were sharing larger apartments in the neighborhood. I relished the private time that small apartment afforded Sharon and me. But after Fred's murder, our earlier and casually expressed near-certainty that we would not live past thirty-five—something we talked about with student audiences and in our more private, thoughtful conversations with each other—became far less casual and easy to say. Our small apartment became as much of a trap and a target as it was a refuge. I grew determined not to go quietly if some ugly and violent part of the government came through the door. With the help of a friend or two, I got a shotgun, which I knew was the best close-quarter defensive weapon, and kept it loaded by the side of our bed for many, many nights that December.

By Christmas time, that feeling of dread and imminent danger had dissipated. That was due as much to the continued dullness of the ever-present trial as it was to any new, more grounded understanding of the actual dangers we faced. Sharon and I flew to New York for a break on a long holiday weekend. We stayed with a friend, a professional photographer, who took pictures of us as we sat naked, hugging with small electric holiday lights strung through our tousled hair. Sharon took the best one of the resulting photos, reproduced it on a 14 x 17 poster with the words "Make a New Year's Revolution Kids! It'll Bring You Closer Together" in a circle around the photograph, and printed a couple hundred copies. After we returned to Chicago, we walked along the line of people waiting to get in to see the trial and handed out the posters. People liked them a lot.

To speed things up that January, the judge ordered the trial to continue on Saturdays. If we weren't already going a little crazy with the mixture of tedium, threat, celebrity, isolation, anger, and a need to continue to respond effectively and be strong, the extra day in that courtroom didn't help. It just confirmed what we already knew—that the trial was quickly winding down.

Before it did, Dave had his bail revoked because of something he said in the courtroom. All of the defendants had spoken out and acted in ways that offended the judge's notion of appropriate courtroom behavior, and he always responded by threatening to revoke our bail. Dave, however, increasingly raised verbal objections to things going on during the trial. Part of it was likely due to the steady accumulation of frustration and outrage over his enforced passivity in the courtroom—after all, Dave was someone who had committed his life to direct action in the face of injustice. But more of it was rooted in Dave's personal history and the values that required him to respond to things that affronted his sense of fairness, honesty, and ethical behavior. And those things were happening almost every day in that courtroom.

In early February, during testimony from one of Chicago's deputy police chiefs, he described what Dave had been doing on the afternoon of August 28. He rightly testified that Dave was at the front of a nonviolent march that led out of Grant Park toward the Loop and the Hilton, but he then said that Dave had gone off with a smaller group that was carrying the Vietcong flag. He also suggested that Dave, of all people, had participated in the later violence on Michigan Avenue.

Dave burst out, "Oh, bullshit!" He added that he would be happy to argue about the differences between what he stood for and what the deputy police chief stood for, but it was not right to make things up like that. The judge, instead of issuing a warning, excused the jury and immediately ended Dave's bail. Dave was then taken through the side door that led to the holding cells. He spent the rest of the trial commuting each day between Cook County Jail and the courtroom.

That night the rest of us were unable to agree on how we should respond to what had just happened. Should we act in ways that would force the judge to revoke our bails as well? That would show our solidarity with Dave and serve as another clear sign the trial was a cruel political hoax. Or should we stay focused on the jury and our appeals for public support, using the final summations and then mobilizing demonstrations and other actions while the jury deliberated? Tom was furious in his tight and determined way; he argued for a straightforward focus on the jury and presenting our case in the courtroom. Abbie and Jerry adamantly demanded immediate, loud, and direct confrontation, a spectacle that would savagely confront the judge. Tom, Jerry, and Abbie would not back down, and the lawyers were powerless. Rennie helped negotiate the kind of solution we often enough fell back on—mostly leaving it up to individuals to decide things for themselves. One thing we did agree on— any confrontations should happen as soon as we got into the courtroom, leaving the lawyers ready to continue the case afterward. The next morning, Jerry and Abbie showed up in court together wearing black judge's robes. When they were told to remove the robes, they were wearing Chicago City Police shirts under them. Both Jerry and Abbie shouted abuse at the judge; Abbie added insults in Yiddish. But if the intent was to have their bail revoked, it failed. The judge all but ignored them and simply ordered the trial to proceed.

For a few more days it did. Finally, at the beginning of the second week in February, both the prosecution and defense lawyers made their final summations to the jury. And in a completely anticipated way—despite the earlier, much more positive outcomes predicted by several smart, leftish, reputable, and wonderful constitutional lawyers—we all went to jail as soon as the jury went off to deliberate our guilt or innocence.

The jurors were barely out of the jury box on February 14 when the judge took up the matter of our behavior in his courtroom. He began counting off the number of times each one of us had been in contempt of his court. He attached jail time, which we would begin serving immediately, to each count. One by one, we each had the chance to say something in response to being sentenced. Everybody was eloquent and politically strong and righteous. Some spectators cried. So did some of our staff in the courtroom. So did Bill Kunstler.

One of the oddest things about the process, which ended up lasting two days, was that we all pretty well knew the contempt charges were coming. And even after it started— Dave was the first in line, then Rennie—we sat around the table and waited our turn to go to jail. It's not like we hadn't considered other possible outcomes. I had certainly thought some about them. But leaving, escaping, going underground, and still somehow staying politically active and relevant didn't seem like it was a very realistic alternative. Getting away might not have been so terribly difficult, but staying away while still being politically effective seemed harder.

I suppose we all tried to hold on to the notion that somehow or other, after a reasonable amount of time, we'd be out on bail while everything was being appealed to higher courts. We wanted to believe what all the smart constitutional lawyers were telling us. But I don't want to minimize the catastrophic sense we all shared of the vicious, brutal politics that seemed to be emerging in America, and the possibility that going to jail might be more dangerous and more final than we might have believed.

One of the few physical objects from that time that I have managed to hang on to provides a time-warp window into that sense of political danger and brutality. It's a note from Sharon that she wrote on a borrowed business card and passed to me while I was waiting to be called up in front of the judge to hear how bad a boy I'd been, and how long I'd go to jail for being naughty in his courtroom.

Sharon was always a little dramatic, but the note certainly reflects the feelings of dread that sometimes haunted all of us, particularly while we were waiting to go to jail that day: "From the first American Revolution till now we have struggled to free ourselves and our brothers. I shall not bend in the face of this when we so greatly need the courage for armed resistance." There was a double-underlined "Love" at the bottom of the note. A little overwrought perhaps, but it was a viewpoint she certainly shared with others.

In the meantime, defendants were being carted off to jail. I loved it that as Abbie was going through the door to the holding cells, he shouted out with a huge grin, "Prison reform is the next important political issue!" My own comments were a little more long-winded, and they were mostly aimed at the judge. After all those months—all the testimony, arguments, and shouting—he still couldn't seem to fully understand how the group of us, who had all sorts of university degrees and who, as he actually said to Tom, "could do very well in this system," went so badly off track. He seemed intrigued by my connection to Northwestern University, where I still had my doctoral research grant, in part because years before, he had been a faculty member there. There was even a plaque with his name on it in an auditorium at the Law School. I grinned as I happily reported, and then reconfirmed when he asked whether it was true, that the students had ripped the plaque off the wall. As I walked to the door that led to the cells, I was laughing too hard to notice how the judge reacted.

———

At first, the fools at Cook County Jail split us up, sending each of us to different floors in the general population cell blocks. I suppose they did that with the expectation that us white boys would be hassled or hurt by a population of mostly nonwhite prisoners. But they failed to take into account that many of those prisoners had plenty of extra time of their hands to watch the TV news, and they'd seen the group of us publicly crapping on the courts and justice system, the same system that had put those guys in jail.

We all almost immediately ended up standing on tabletops in the common areas of each floor, giving loud, strong, and defiant speeches to applause and much cheering and laughter. That quickly got us removed from the general population and into the isolation cells that were on the special floor block reserved for in transient federal prisoners. Before we were each moved into our own solitary cells, they asked when we'd each like our hour or so out of the cells. Of course everybody picked the time the evening news was on. Each night, we'd watch a TV hanging from the ceiling the demonstrations against the trial that were happening at one college campus or another, loudly and laughingly claiming individual credit if we had spoken at that particular school.

We were locked in those solitary cells for four days while we waited for the jury's decision. On February 19, they came back with their verdict. Later interviews with members of the jury described back and forth arguments and negotiations between four members of the jury who thought none of us were guilty of much of anything and the other eight members, some of whom thought we were all guilty of everything. So they compromised, which they'd always been implicitly invited to do by the complicated indictments of two charges apiece for the seven defendants. In that compromise, the jurors could trade away their actual beliefs about the guilt or innocence of individual defendants just so they could end the thing and make their own escape from the trial and their five-month-long sequestration.

We all stood up around the old defendants' table to hear the verdicts. Nobody was guilty of conspiracy. John and I were acquitted of everything, but Dave, Tom, Rennie, Abbie, and Jerry were each guilty on their individual "substantive counts"—the speeches they gave. John cried at the idea of being separated from the others. I was half-stunned and speechless, caught between an instant of confusion and disbelief at having escaped the most immediate and worst personal threat, and knowing that none of it—the political struggle or the trial— was really over. The judge had already said we were dangerous men. He denied us bail on the convictions and the contempt charges. We all went back to jail.

We were still being kept on the federal transient prisoner floor, and as we watched the news coverage of the demonstrations and rioting that took place in reaction to the verdicts, some of our earliest discussions were about the reasons for the jury's split decision. The most benign was that John and I had been thrown in as representatives of students and academics, and that we were lucky to escape. A less benign theory personally hurt me the most because I thought it might be true. That John and I were included as a deliberate ploy, reducing the legitimacy and "deservedness" of our indictments. Our inclusion gave the jury a way to compromise while still being able to convict the more famous among us. And then, when we were found not guilty, those same verdicts could be used to argue that the trial and jury decision was fair and that the others were justly accused and convicted. It wasn't until a couple of weeks later that Morty Stavis, one of the founders of the Center for Constitutional Rights, offered me a less deflating and guilt-inducing reason for why John and I had been indicted with the others. He suggested that without the inclusion of our incendiary device charges, it was all just speaking and association that was protected by the First Amendment, a case that even a quasi-controlled federal grand jury might have been reluctant to press forward on. That would have made it far more likely that people from the more traditional legal establishment would have mobilized in opposition to the trial. I liked that reasoning a lot better, but I thought, both then and now, that my inclusion in the trial was likely the result of some perverse combination of all three reasons.

In jail the next day, they took us all together to the prison barber shop to cut off everybody's hair. We were half-lined up, just crowded in a bunch in a narrow entryway to the small room. Abbie yelled that we should fight, force them to pay a price, that our hair was a symbol of our freedom and of everything we believed and that we couldn't just acquiesce. Two big guards had to hold Abbie's arms down and keep him in the chair while the barber did his thing. None of the rest of us made much of a struggle at all. But Abbie was right. The Cook County sheriff displayed piles of our hair as a glorious war trophy at a Republican political fundraising dinner one night that week to his donors' wild applause.

But then, as all the fancy lawyers who had helped us at one time or another had promised, we were all released after an appeals court disagreed with Judge Hoffman and ordered us freed on bail during our appeals of the contempt charges and the convictions. We were in jail for another nine days after the verdicts before we got out.

Those last days in jail were filled with group meetings with the lawyers who were working on the appeal. They always assured us they were certain we wouldn't be in jail very much longer. There was mostly bad food and lonely nights. We were still encouraged by news about the continuing demonstrations supporting us around the country, but in our meetings with the lawyers, and in our conversations when we were out of the cells together, I began to feel small but noticeable distances opening up between us. John and I had been acquitted of the felony charges, and while the initial appeals focused on overturning Judge Hoffman's denial of bail, in our meetings with the lawyer, John and I never initiated any questions about the broader appeal against the convictions, though the others occasionally did.

Except it was more than that. The old political and cultural differences, as well as the ego competitions between us, began to reemerge. Jerry and Abbie disagreed with one another on what to do after we were released. Jerry insisted we should all immediately go back on the road to college campuses to build some sort of national organization off of the energy and rioting the trial had unleashed. Abbie and I talked a bit about some small hotel he knew on a quiet beach in Puerto Rico that sounded like a better place to spend some time after we got out of jail. Tom didn't think either of those options made any sense, but he was more direct in his criticism of Jerry than Abbie's plan. Rennie wrote that he remembers asking us to stay in jail until "our staff" raised additional money for bail in an act of solidarity with other, poorer inmates, and Tom wrote that we helped bail out other inmates at Cook County, but I don't remember that really happening. We might have been heroes at the moment, but we weren't saints. We stayed in jail only until the appeals court let us out. And we did have a substantial amount of money left over; our staff office transferred $30,000—well over $130,000 in today's money— to the Center for Constitutional Rights, which would be doing all our appeal work.

When we left jail, it was with a level of national recognition and celebrity that none of us had experienced—even Tom, Rennie, Abbie, and Jerry, who had already achieved notable public attention for their political work before the trial. Worse, our celebrity often made the media brand us with a public identity as "leaders." But media acclamation and individual "leadership" both ran counter to the communal values of the movement we all grew up in, and they were treated with increasing suspicion and hostility in the evolving radical politics that was such a big part of our lives. Adjusting to life in the aftermath of such a monumental event would not be easy for any of the defendants.

Chapter 5
Picking Up the Pieces

After the trial, I left Chicago. Despite my initial intention to stay and work politically, the police's continuing and conspicuous interest in me made it impossible. It was dangerous for me and anyone I might work with. I had to leave. And so I asked for help from some of the faculty at Northwestern, and they arranged a teaching job for me in the sociology department at Rutgers University in New Jersey.

I certainly wasn't going to live in New Jersey, though. So Sharon and I rented a first-floor studio apartment in a converted townhouse on Dean Street in a Brooklyn neighborhood that was already moving quickly toward gentrification, even if it hadn't completely arrived there yet. I reconnected with some political friends and started commuting by car two or three days a week to teach at Rutgers.

The nice thing about that car ride out of Brooklyn—across a bridge into New Jersey and then onto I-95 and down to New Brunswick—was that there was plenty of time to think. First up was how long I was going to be able to last teaching at Rutgers. The sociology department I was working in was being built by Irving Louis Horowitz, a friend of some people I had studied with at Northwestern. Irving also happened to be the editor of a paperback book collection of writings by anarchists that I had read. He definitely wasn't an anarchist, but he was smart and aggressive. He wanted to put together a group of smart, mostly left-leaning (or at least liberal) sociologists in the Livingston campus of Rutgers to see what might happen. It was 1970, and all sorts of interesting political things were going on in the world, so why not see what might happen in a newly established sociology department that nobody had the time to pay much attention to yet?

I suppose if I had just kept teaching a couple of classes, if I had attended faculty meetings more often and worked on finishing my dissertation in a more timely way, I might still be there. But it didn't work out. While I was teaching at Rutgers, I was also living a couple of other lives in New York. And a sidebar event in one of those lives would cause Irving's sociology department a little more grief than they might have expected or wanted.

For the time being, though, I settled into teaching a class to undergraduates on "social change," which was fitting given what I had just been through and what I looked and sounded like. The lectures were fairly crowded with earnest young men and women, and I'd sometimes spend time with them after class as they tried to work out how they might be more politically effective. In the spring at some point, I suggested that as an alternative to a couple of lectures I'd miss because I'd be away, some people in the class might consider joining me at the May Day anti-war demonstrations in DC.

Rennie had helped put the protest together. It had been designed to take place after nearly two weeks of anti-war demonstrations in the capital, including a gathering of 500,000 people on the Mall and a protest where the Vietnam Vets Against the War threw back their service medals toward the steps of the Capitol Building. The planned May Day actions were Rennie's leap outside of the more traditional anti-war organizations and their slightly passive accumulations of ever greater numbers of people who would show up to demonstrate their opposition to the war. It was supposed to be all about affinity groups—relatively small numbers of people who already knew and trusted one another—using nonviolent resistance in hit-and-run tactics to snarl traffic on bridges and roadways and "close down the government." More than a few of my students went down to DC, and after the rally, I gave a fairly uninhibited interview to the campus newspaper. In the background of the photo of me that accompanied my rant, there was the big red poster of a strident Lenin that hung on my office wall.

Surprisingly, neither of those things got me in trouble. The problem arose out of two other things going on in my life. The first was partly a consequence of those long, thoughtful drives from Brooklyn to New Jersey. If you took a look at the Black Panthers, the Young Lords, and all the other emerging ethnic and racially based liberation movements, then read some of Mao's writings on the role of revolutionary nationalism in the broader revolutionary struggle, and then added a bit of Brooklyn into the mix, the notion of Revolutionary Jewish Nationalism suddenly started to make a lot of sense.

Mao had always been a China-focused revolutionary nationalist, diverging from traditional Marxist and Leninist theory, and as his broader movement based on the peasantry grew, he had welcomed minority ethnic groups in China to initially form their own radical nationalisms and group aspirations. He always knew that those separate minority nationalisms would be subsumed within the broader revolutionary struggle. Along those same lines, the rise and legitimacy of separate racial, ethnic, gender, and LGBTQ-identified groupings within the progressive, radical political movement in the US was undeniable. And if Jews—as a separate, self-identified group with revolutionary goals—had been important and diverse parts of earlier revolutionary movements, especially in Russia, why couldn't they be an equally legitimate, self-identified revolutionary group within the US? It made sense to me. And besides, it would be a sort of nasty fun to openly and loudly remind American Jews of their separateness they usually didn't talk about in public, and their legacy and commitments to social justice.

At first with just a few friends (including Wolfe Lowenthal, who I had remained close to after the 1968 demonstrations in Chicago), we formed a collective to think about and build a new movement. We grew quickly by recruiting several young people who were already associated with other leftist political efforts in New York. Part of that work was to write a graphic-filled broadsheet newspaper called the *Brooklyn Bridge* and distribute it in some high schools. The newspaper preached Revolutionary Jewish Nationalism as a legitimate expression of a group that was oppressed and still discriminated against and that shared the progressive goals of a growing radical movement in America.

The event that more directly contributed to the end of my time at Rutgers, however, was related to my self-indulgence in some of the upsides of being a celebrity in New York City. When you've achieved some degree of notoriety, and you're already floating on the edges of that strange intersection of newspaper reporters, writers, artists, performers, political activists, and the rich in New York City, you get invited to parties. And not just parties south of Fourteenth Street. You get invited to what turn out to be very pleasant places, such as the Dakota.

Built in the 1880s on what is now Seventy-Second and Central Park West, the Dakota was and still is an elegant place for rich and famous people to live. But in the seventies, it was an especially hip destination. It was featured in Tom Wolfe's *New York* magazine cover story about rich liberals gathering to support the Black Panthers. At one particular crowded party, with Andy Warhol dressed all in white and chatting up socialites in the corner, I struck up a conversation with Israel's ambassador to the UN about the informer they had placed in our little Jewish commie/nationalist Brooklyn collective, nodding understandably when he asked, "Wouldn't you?" I didn't notice that a *New York Times* reporter I knew was also listening.

At an uptown party a week or two later, that same reporter cornered me, reminding me about my conversation with the ambassador and asking what I was doing politically. To avoid talking about the collective, which certainly didn't need any more bumps in the road or public notice—Bob Dylan had shown up looking for me when I wasn't at the collective's small office, totally freaking out the kids who were there at the time—I started talking about Rutgers. Fully aware we were on the record, I praised the young men and women I had been meeting with privately to discuss their still emerging and different ways of acting politically, and about the possible invention of a new sort of Communist Party. I can't deny that I knew that was the quote he would use if he wrote something.

While I was not the primary focus of the *New York Times Magazine* piece that he wrote, my comment was included. I barely had a chance to read the article that Sunday morning when the phone rang. It was Irving Horowitz telling me I had to come to a specially called departmental meeting the next morning. It seemed that the head of the New Jersey State Police had read the article and had gotten a little upset, though that's probably a bit of an understatement. I don't remember whether he had actually sent his ripped-up paycheck to the governor, or if he was just threatening to do so because he couldn't tolerate being paid by the same state that was also paying a commie instructor at Rutgers. Not surprisingly, the governor called the president of the university, and the president of the university called Irving to ask what the hell was going on in his department.

The department meeting on Monday went about as one might expect. There were many expressions of concern about academic freedom and some reluctant agreement that the department would have to defend me. No questions were asked about whether I was actually building a new Communist Party. Irving did angrily ask me at some point why the hell I had spoken with the reporter, and I couldn't come up with a decent reply. In the end, I told them I wasn't interested in another public political brawl—something I had more experience with than they did—and I certainly didn't want one over liberal notions of academic freedom. So I told them I'd leave at the end of the spring semester. These were all good people. Most of them had recently moved to that forsaken corner of New Jersey, bought homes, and were constructing their lives with the expectation of staying at the university for a while. Did I read some relief in their eyes when I answered the few half-hearted objections to my decision? Of course I did. But so what?

I was then stuck with a perfectly reasonable question: How was I going to make a living? Would I write a book? Find some other way to cash in on the lingering residue of fame? Abbie and Jerry were definitely riding that particular train. And while I admit that being with them a couple of times at John and Yoko's place in the West Village remains the type of visual memory that will stick in the back of my head forever, Jerry and Abbie's frenetic running around made me a little nauseous. Earlier, Tom had been thrown out of his West Coast Red Family collective—he was too famous, too dominant, too much a politician. Then, after the DC May Day demonstrations, Rennie seemed to have collapsed into himself. He traveled to India, had a vision he later told me about that involved a flock of black birds—I'll avoid all judgments here, though I admit my old clinical social work diagnostic antenna popped up—and then he joined up with an Indian guru. None of that suggested anything particularly promising about making a living on the political front.

So I talked to a lot of people about possible work. I had become connected to a law firm in a friendly way—it had been established by twin brothers who had initially been denied entrance to the New York Bar because of their lefty backgrounds. Someone who worked there was married to a woman who had a friend who happened to be looking for a social worker at the men's shelter in lower Manhattan. I met this friend, Ellen Sundheimer, applied for the job, and was hired. The medical director wanted to know why I wanted to work there. He suspected I had a potentially terrible plan that somehow involved down-and-out alcoholics and revolution, but I just laughed. After a few meetings about treatment plans, and a few rounds with the staff guys who rode the streets around the Bowery picking up endangered, sick, and hurting drunks, I was accepted as an unlikely but reasonable enough new staff member.

For most of the next year, that's what I did. I was still living a split life: there was my life in the Bowery as a clinical supervisor with a small staff who was trying to help men living on the street, and then there was my life in Brooklyn with Sharon and my time hanging out in lower Manhattan with political friends. We worried about people we knew who were caught up in the Attica riots, or other people who were on the run from bombings, serious robberies, and shootings. We also worried about how we could continue to be political without joining some loud or secretive faction, without bombing anything or going underground, or worse, just continuing to hang out with famous people.

At this point, the legitimation, and even the celebration of deliberate acts of violence against symbolic and actual representatives of government authority and capitalist exploitation had grown far past the "Days of Rage" in 1969. That simple, pride-filled acceptance of fighting in the streets had included the bombing of a statue in Haymarket Square that commemorated the police who had been killed in an 1886 demonstration over labor rights. Now the use of violence by the Left seemed to be everywhere. It was in the news and in conversations and arguments with friends. The political justifications varied a bit between different factions or groups of individual actors. Some people wanted to recruit working-class youth and show by example what actions were now required to support revolutionary change in America. Others wanted to exact a visible cost in the US for supporting the war; to expropriate the money that was needed to support a necessarily more violent struggle against racism; or to fight in real solidarity with the Vietnamese and other "oppressed peoples."

I was crazy with worry for the people I knew who were being tempted by the seductive simplicity that politically motivated violence was something definite, concrete, and immediately doable, that it was the method that would quickly bring about the changes in America we all knew were necessary. I didn't believe that episodic, isolated acts of violence would help change anything for the better. But I couldn't see or offer any alternative other than the unglamorous, grinding daily work that was required to sustain a long, arduous political struggle with no certain victories. And even I wasn't able to mobilize the personal energy and commitment to do such work. "The Brooklyn Bridge" collective collapsed in part because of the tension and conflicts over how violence fit into its politics.

Like everybody else, I made some ridiculous choices. The worst was when I thought Jerry and Abbie's idea about going to Miami for the 1972 Democratic National Convention sounded perfectly reasonable. Of course it made no sense whatsoever, except perhaps as an expression of their desperation to stay politically relevant. But I felt the same way. For the first time in years, there didn't seem to be anything I was willing or capable of doing that would advance the political ideals I was still committed to. And reaching back to the setting and tactics that had propelled us into the spotlight at least offered us something to do.

The differences between Chicago and Miami were stark. In Miami, instead of the righteous anger and confrontations with state power and repression that defined Chicago, we were covertly and laughingly given passes to the convention floor, courtesy of a very different Democratic Party and the young McGovern delegates. The grown-up crazies like Abbie Hoffman, Jerry Rubin, Ed Sanders, me, and a couple of others stayed at a beat-up hotel in Miami Beach, while kids lazed around in a couple of small parks, often indulging in brain-rotting quaaludes. We political celebrities went to parties on those small, private islands between Miami and Miami Beach, and had our own parties at the hotel.

"Degeneracy" is the word that still seems the most apt descriptor of what went on in Miami. There were a lot of women and a lot of drugs and very little politics. The bar at our hotel had a large picture window that looked out to the deep end of the hotel's pool, and you could drink and watch friends and lovers frolic in the water. At a party where different drugs were served on a rotating Lazy Susan, I was offered an opportunity to join the hosts in their dope importing and distribution business. Before I passed out, I definitely considered it.

That was the turning point for me. Too many friends had gone way, way off the rails, insisting as they flew off into an unknown and darkening sky that they were all doing important political work. I managed to get back to Brooklyn. I was finally as done as I could be with celebrity, with pills, powders, and hallucinogenics, and with what had become grotesque, pretend politics. One afternoon, I walked over to a diner I knew off of Flatbush Avenue, took a seat in a booth, and carefully and thoughtfully tore one page at a time out of my personal telephone notebook. I burned each of them in a tin ashtray on the table. Every page. Every name.

It was a decent start, but it wasn't enough by a long shot. I started seeing a therapist, who quickly diagnosed me with acute depression, and I began the long emotional climb out of a once vibrant but now decaying political world that had been all I had mostly cared about for ten years. Without very much drama or disagreement, Sharon and I decided that our time together had come to an end, and I moved into my own apartment in Brooklyn Heights. I was trying as hard as I could to create some space for myself, away from the politics that, for me and many of my old friends, had become ever more desperate, dangerous, and harder to tolerate. It mostly worked out.

I stayed in therapy and kept on as a social worker for a while. My boss, Ellen, who was married to a successful commodity trader, was a smart, competent, tough, and determined woman. A doctor's daughter, her politics were more a mix of suburban New Jersey, Jewish upper-middle-class liberal intentions than any thought-through notions of how America might be changed. After I moved to my new apartment, she and I almost haphazardly became occasional lovers. Her lack of serious politics was a welcome relief, and over time, our relationship became more serious. When she began the process of divorcing her husband, we started living together in Brooklyn Heights and eventually moved to Greenwich Village to start fresh.

Though my public profile had diminished considerably since the trial, it wasn't like I dropped off the face of the planet. Some of the performers and writing staff of *Saturday Night Live* lived in our building; other people were pretty consistently involved with the gay bar and street scene down by the nearby piers; still others were active with the Village Independent Democrats; and a couple of the saner writers I knew lived there. But while I still saw some political people, I did my best to avoid most of the others.

After two years together, and an earlier, simple uncontested divorce from Adelle that simply ratified our long separation, Ellen and I got married. I'd love to say that it was a wonderful start to a new and wonderful life, but it was really just me grasping at something, anything, that offered the possibility of relief from shuffling through the ashes of what my life had been. For the next few years, I continued to live an odd, if somewhat more settled, life. I left my job and collected unemployment benefits for a while. I got work as a consultant and staff trainer with small nonprofits that were providing direct services to people who were poor. I managed to find some people who knew some other people and did some evaluative research for the city's Addiction Services Agency (giving appreciative cheers to the statistics courses I had to take at Northwestern). I finished my dissertation, collecting another public credential that might help me earn a living somewhere, somehow.

I was invited and joined a men's consciousness raising group, one of the healthier responses to the changes the women's movement was bringing to all our lives. I had avoided being publicly denounced and shamed for sexist values and behaviors, not because it wasn't deserved, but mostly because I wasn't prominent enough. It also helped that I was part of a group of more visible and rewarding targets like Abbie, Jerry, and Tom, who absorbed most of the righteous fury directed our way. In the men's group, I initially knew only one person, but after a while, and for the first time, the thing that came to bind me together emotionally with other men wasn't just politics.

Things with some of my well-known friends definitely weren't going quite as well. Abbie had been charged with the intent to sell cocaine in the late summer of 1973. I remember sitting with Allen Ginsburg at a small table at the back of a downtown bar at a fundraiser for Abbie's legal expenses, talking and feeling sad about it all. Allen tried hard to make me feel better, or at least be easier with it. Then Abbie came over for a private conversation about what I might happen to know about diamonds and about financing a more private life than the one he was used to living. Afterward, Allen was as sad as I was. By the spring of 1974, Abbie had jumped bail and gone underground. Not too very long afterward, a bearded, ultra-Orthodox Jewish man, traditionally dressed in a dark suit and large fedora hat, passed me on a street in the Village and quietly called out my name. It was Abbie, and he and I were able to relax and talk a bit at my apartment. He was still in the "happy-to-have-gotten-away" phase of the strange new life he was constructing for himself, so seeing him was sort of wonderful and sad at the same time.

Jerry—who like Abbie, and unlike me, had accepted the burdens and glories of ferocious notoriety and public leadership—had also been trapped in the drastically changing, withering political world. He was even unable to stay in New York. He fled in late 1972 to San Francisco in what I've always believed was an honest, hopeful, and desperate effort to save himself. Out west, he truly and completely jumped into the then expanding New Age world of Est, diet, exercise, Rolfing, vitamins, meditation, and self-awareness. It wouldn't be his last effort at transformation and salvation.

In the early fall of 1976, one of my new friends in the men's group offered a stepping stone out of the stagnating, shallow, and boring recovery life I had been wallowing in. Gary was a well-connected and solid political operative who had worked on Robert Kennedy's presidential campaign. He was active in New York City politics, and he excelled in making cross-connections between labor unions and the Democratic Party. At that time, he was working with the Jimmy Carter campaign in Ohio and worrying about Carter's chances. He asked whether I'd want to work in getting out the vote in a congressional district or two in the Cleveland metro area. He told me he really needed the help and that nobody would know or figure out who I used to be. So I went, and Ellen came along to help. I remember telling her that when the folks we were going to be working with asked her who she was, they were really asking her if she was Jewish. If she just told them she was from New York, that would be a sufficient answer.

Eventually, Hawaii gave the electoral victory to Carter a little earlier than the late returns from Ohio would have, but the senior campaign people in Ohio still had some drag in Carter's emerging administration. Gary got a job at the Labor Department, and after a while, I was invited to join an odd collection of ex-McCarthy types and other liberal folks down the street from the White House at ACTION, which was then responsible for the Peace Corps, VISTA, and other voluntary citizen activities. Ellen and I and our brand-new baby moved out of New York to a townhouse in regentrifying Capitol Hill, and it was fun for a while. Fairly early on in my time there, Illinois Congressman Bob Michel, a member of the Republican leadership, publicly denounced me in a speech on the floor of the House of Representatives. He was pissed that a horrible person like me would be hired to work for the new Democratic administration. The supportive counter to that by Sam Brown—who was the head of ACTION, had been the youth coordinator for Senator McCarthy's 1968 presidential campaign, and had also testified at our trial—was to have me immediately tag along to a major meeting being held in the Old Executive Office Building next door to the White House. The basic theory was that we'd show them it wasn't the 1950s anymore, and that some people who might have looked and smelled a bit like commies weren't necessarily irretrievably bad or horrible people. It would have worked a little better symbolically if I had been allowed into the building like everybody else. Instead, I was very politely told I'd have to wait to be personally escorted to the meeting. I don't remember which security service had put a hold on me that first time—maybe it was the FBI—but several of them would take turns doing it over the coming months.

The work became more interesting after I began to understand that a lot of the emerging environmental and liberal nonprofit groups operating in Washington were scrambling to build mass constituencies, using direct mail, to free themselves from the whims and constraints of their few wealthy donors and supporting charitable foundations. I figured out that if I learned some new skills, I might be able to help those nonprofits broaden the base of support for political policies I agreed with, and even earn a living at it.

Through a family connection of Ellen's, I got a job at one of the early direct mail consulting firms. In the late seventies, there wasn't a lot of affordable personal data available for use in nonprofit fundraising. Back then, "personalization" just meant putting somebody's name on the front page of a letter and referencing their name and address as often as possible: "Mr. Jones, if you and all your neighbors on Colfax Avenue just decided to contribute. . ." Client-facing roles didn't seem like a natural fit for me at first, but I lasted long enough with the firm that had hired me to learn the basics of the art and trade. With my old grad school background in statistics and data analytics, I learned I was good at reading test mailing results and polling data. I started my own business and got some clients: the Environmental Defense Fund, a few other progressive nonprofits, a governor's race, and some members of Congress.

For a while life seemed okay. I was doing explicit political work again, and if the politics weren't very much like they used to be, they were at least mostly progressive politics that were pointed in the right direction. And that seemed to be all anybody could reasonably hope for anymore. Ellen and I had another daughter, and then a son, and if she and I were no longer getting along as well as we might have wished, it was just how things were. I hadn't forgotten my old political hopes and dreams, but I had learned to mostly push them off to one side. I couldn't really do anything about them, and every time I really thought about them for too long, I just made myself crazy with either guilt or regret. In much the same way, I forced away notions of passion and lasting romance. I wasn't particularly happy, and in client meetings where I should have known better, I was occasionally more sarcastic or cynical than I should have been. But I told myself that the work and my kids were enough.

It was Tom Foley who did me in. My initial work for him was simply to raise whatever I could in campaign contributions through mail appeals in his home district in eastern Washington State. All his real campaign money came from the large corporations, national business associations, and lobbyists that generously supported anybody who was even slightly important in Congress. Tom was already pretty important in Congress, so the money I helped raise was mostly just for a cover story—it was local support he could talk about on trips back to his district if anybody in the press asked. Two years later, I was doing the same work for him, but it was 1988 and Tom was suddenly the Speaker of the House. I soon found out what happens when you're a newish consultant to a very important politician in the terribly self-involved, grasping, and gossipy small town of political Washington, DC. Basically your phone never stops ringing.

Up until then, I liked just about everybody I had worked with. But I was not at all prepared to join the big leagues. It would mean hiring many new employees, or more likely getting connected to one or another of the already established big direct response or political consulting firms. Instead, I talked with Ellen about going back to New York. I called one of my clients up there—the Anti-Defamation League—and told them it would be cheaper for them to hire me full-time than to continue paying consulting fees to my firm. They happily agreed, and Ellen and I made plans for the move back.

I hugged and kissed all my clients goodbye; I temporarily moved into a friend's apartment just north of Fourteenth Street on the west side and started working for the ADL. For a while, I flew back to DC each weekend to see Ellen and the kids and help prepare for everybody to move. But that part of it didn't work out.

It wasn't very long; the weather was still nice enough for me to walk across town up to Forty-Sixth by the UN where the ADL had its offices. Ellen announced that she'd changed her mind about coming back to New York, and she insisted I return to DC. I tried to explain why that couldn't work. First, I had made a serious commitment to the ADL, which had invested a noticeable amount of additional money and staff into their direct response program since I had gotten there. Second, after you say goodbye in DC, it's hard for anybody, especially independent consultants like me, to just reappear and expect all the clients to come back. Finally, despite our three children, she and I hadn't been getting along for quite a long time. So I refused to go back.

After a bitter and expensive time with divorce attorneys instead of political ones, and family court instead of criminal court, I wasn't married any longer. I kept working for the ADL and met Karen Mann there. She was one of the ADL's fundraisers for major events. She was drop-dead gorgeous, always with sophisticated makeup and clothes. Soon enough, she and I were living together in her place in Midtown on the East Side. Karen was about as straight and apolitical as I supposed a person could be while still being able to have a coherent conversation with the other adults I knew, but I didn't care. Jerry had moved back to the city, too, and he and I saw one another occasionally. He was either doing his stockbroker thing or was already promoting his social networks. In a lot of ways, he had become even more apolitical than Karen was.

After Karen and I got married, we bought an apartment with some money that came in from my grandfather's estate after my mother died. It was in Tudor City, overlooking the East River, across from the UN, and a five-minute walk to the ADL offices. We had a daughter, and then another, and I soon figured out that the money side of living in the city wasn't going to work out with us both employed by a nonprofit organization. Karen, who had grown up in a big house in Connecticut, handled everything about getting us out of the city and buying a place in the suburbs.

I worked at the ADL for fifteen years. They were good years, helping in the fight against racism, bigotry, and anti-Semitism. I heard stories from the older men in the field offices who had risked themselves and their families against the Klan, and there were other stories from some of the younger men and women who were building anti-bigotry campaigns in their cities. Those stories, the all too often eruptions of hate and right-wing extremist violence during the nineties, and the increasingly sophisticated data and communication tools available to me, all helped to vastly expand the individual donor base supporting the ADL, which noticeably increased its small dollar contributions every year.

It came to an end in a not unexpected way, and it was nothing terrible. One of the constant questions moderately sized national nonprofit organizations face is just how long they can pay both an expensive internal staff and expensive third-party consultants to run their direct response program. After all those years, the ADL program was well established, and nobody seemed to have a magic wand to suddenly make it more wonderful. There was also a new VP of Communication who wanted to make an impression by making changes. Why not let a more junior person just oversee the ongoing thing and let the consultants, who you were paying anyway, run it? Having been on the other side of the staff versus consultants dilemma, I certainly understood when my boss decided he could live without me. I told him not to feel bad, as long as he gave me a really generous separation package. He did just that.

A little while later, I started building a similar direct response program at an international disaster relief and health-focused humanitarian aid organization called Americares. It was based in Connecticut, so it was a lot easier getting to work. I was there for about ten years, until a newly hired Senior VP of Development made the same decision about me that the ADL had. The separation package wasn't as generous, but I was in my mid-seventies, so I decided I'd try slowing down a little.

After looking at some places in Florida where we might live together, Karen decided she preferred to stay in Connecticut without me, and finally decided that a divorce made better sense. So now I live alone, in warm weather and in pretty regular contact with my six children. The kids have been kind and forgiving enough of my earlier abandonments and failures to still allow me into their lives, but I only have intermittent contact with their mothers.

On particularly nice days, I admit I am sometimes tempted to take Colin Harrison's words in *You Belong to Me* to heart when he suggests, "no one is interested in the opinions of an old man sitting next to a pool," and that "history has moved on, left [me] at the station holding a heavy suitcase and a worthless ticket." Except political history really hasn't moved on that far. Inequality and oppression of every sort—racism, sexism, and war—are still front and center in our politics today.

Now they share the stage with globalization, terrorism, the struggles over immigration and citizenship, environmental disasters, and climate change. And we again have a president and federal government to be terribly worried about. So learning how to act politically and to more effectively resist the powers of a state that protects the wealthy continues to be vitally important. And wondering what the hell one should do, besides finding a safe corner somewhere and hiding with a few friends, is as much of a real question now as it was when I was younger and running in the streets.

Chapter 6

Different Times, Same Fight

The trial of the Chicago Seven (or the Chicago Eight Conspiracy) wasn't anywhere near the first time the government had used its prosecutors and courts to punish political dissent on the left. The mobilization of local and federal authorities, state-sanctioned violence, police, laws, and the formal and time-consuming procedures of the court were all weapons that had regularly been used to threaten, attack, and coerce individuals and organizations who opposed existing arrangements of government and economic power.

But our trial caused a bigger stir than most. In part, that might have been an accident of timing and the misplaced enthusiasm of newly elected Republicans who were determined to act as quickly as they could against their perceived enemies. So the trial was rushed into being, and it ended up almost perfectly placed in the middle of a rapidly growing, near-cresting wave of distrust toward the government, public anger about the continuing war, and a broadly felt, if not clearly articulated, yearning for something better. It was all very much a part of the sixties, which is a time that's hard to describe, even for people who lived through them.

No single book, article, blog post—or even hours of music, video, and interviews—have been able to adequately sum up the sixties. They can't. For example, Ken Burns and Lynn Novick's ten-part TV series on the Vietnam War was eighteen hours long, and it still generated plenty of legitimate criticism about what was missed and what was glossed over, and that film was "just" about the war. Vietnam was certainly a significant part of the context surrounding all our lives, but it wasn't everything—not everything by quite a bit. The failure to satisfactorily grab an intellectual and emotional hold of the sixties can partly be blamed on the simple fact that there was so much going on.

If you google "the sixties," you get more than ninety-six million hits. Do the same the same for the seventies and eighties and you get forty-nine million and forty-four million respectively. And when people say "the sixties," it's not always even clear what years they're actually referring to. Do the sixties start with Kennedy's election in 1960? Maybe with the Greensboro sit-ins that started much earlier that same year? The Montgomery Bus Boycott began in 1955; surely that was the start of something. In his book on the sixties, Tom Brokaw claims they start with the 1963 March on Washington and Martin Luther King's "I Have a Dream" speech. But then when did the sixties end? Was it in 1970, when National Guard troops killed students at Kent State University and then, ten days later, Mississippi police officers killed students at Jackson State? Or maybe the sixties ended with the 1972 electoral defeat of McGovern and Nixon's reelection.

I don't really think the exact date parameters are that important. After all, there were plenty of hints of what was to come before the actual year of 1960 even got started. And the whirlwind of change and noise from those years didn't fully settle down even after Nixon made his getaway from the Watergate mess by boarding a helicopter on the White House lawn in 1974, a forced smile on his face and his arms raised high with a two-handed V-sign.

To understand that time, and especially its continuing impact on politics in America today, I think you have to start with the children who grew up in the fifties, children who heard family stories that often made them the unintentional heirs of some of the remnants of the radical politics of the thirties and forties. "Red Diaper Babies" was the derogatory, dismissive, and sometimes fearsome label that some observers used to describe these children. But as my own story suggests, it was much broader than that. Many more people, besides just the kids of actual Communist Party members, learned from their families that "politics" was a separate but real thing, that it had once and might again influence people's lives. And we were all living in places that were richer and that seemed freer. It was a world filled with more cars, TVs, and opportunities to learn and try new things without necessarily terrible consequences.

Into that stew of possibilities suddenly came the vivid images on TV and in the newspapers of people who were fighting against racial segregation in the South. That public torrent of pictures and stories announced, over and over again, that individuals acting with moral courage and conviction could create something new by confronting injustice and power. We had all known that was part of America's promise and history, but now we were being shown it might still be true. Those images shook America and began to change it.

What you could see, and what you could talk about with friends, was the fact that people could be moved to act politically by their values, by their sense of what was right and what was wrong. We could see that we could openly fight against what was wrong by joining together with others who recognized the same wrongs. Even more, you could also be part of making America better simply by acting politically, by personally and directly joining in a struggle against injustice.

This was the most important and lasting political lesson of my life. Neither I nor anyone I considered a friend ever questioned the notion that personal political acts are sometimes absolutely required, and that those acts can be and should be motivated by one's values and commitments to social justice. Politics was not only about power and money. It was one of the ways to find, save, and express one's best self. It was a context in which you could declare, promote, act out, and strengthen your most important positive personal values.

I believed it then. I believe it now.

The interesting thing is that although these may seem to be very different times from the politics and commotion and cultural changes of the Sixties, in a few important ways they are very similar. Most people then and now aren't political. The majority of Americans simply try to live normal lives filled with work, family, and friends. Politics is treated like the weather—they know it affects them, but if they're lucky, it doesn't affect them too much, and there is really not much of anything they believe they can do about it anyway. They just live through it and hope for the best. But it was in a similar context in the late fifties and sixties, where most people were living sensible and often hopeful everyday lives, that some young people made a transition to believing that their personal involvement in politics was important, maybe even required.

And now, so many years later, many people are also becoming more directly involved in politics and political work. And some of the initial prompts—just like in the sixties—come from being assaulted by vivid media imagery and stories. There are digital visions of neo-Nazis marching on the streets in an American city, chanting against immigrants, blacks, and Jews, and pictures of crying, angry parents mourning the death of their child who was killed by a police officer for no understandable reason. Those images flash across screens without so much as a commercial break between the stories sometimes. When people have to make snap transitions between different video realities and their own daily lives, it can make them feel a little dizzy; all those brutal images are erupting in the middle of what's supposed to be the settled, comfortable, and ordinary places people live.

Practically no one in cable or internet news intends for any of those stories to provoke anybody to actually become more politically engaged. I'm sure it's quite the opposite. The preference is for people not to take any of it too seriously, to just buy some product or other, or subscribe or follow or click on to the next web page or promoted site. After all, swiping the images away on a phone is pretty easy. And the images people share of their daily lives on Facebook, Twitter, and Instagram can all help distract us from taking those ugly things too seriously. But the music, videos, movies, and digital relationships that are always there can't always shield everybody from worrying or wondering about the repeated, intrusive images and stories about people who are hurting.

Now, often far more quickly than I and many of my friends learned, people understand that engaging in politics is what is required to stop some of the ugliness and suffering. In part, that's because "politics" is harder to avoid now, no matter how much people might be tempted to try. Most television coverage of politics in the fifties and early sixties was almost benign. It certainly was never cruel or savage. But today's often ferocious and loud Republican and Democratic tribal splitting can make it impossible not to see "politics" as an all too visible, divisive force in America. And because all that noise and those images people see of hurt and pain and cruelty either offends their sense of what America should be, or threatens an America they believe needs defending, many people feel compelled to choose a side. They decide to belong to one tribe, and then they act personally and politically to demean and attack the other.

In the early sixties, we knew that there were many people whose values, traditions, and beliefs were very different from our own emerging commitments to racial, social, and economic justice. Early on, they were the people, sometimes family members, who we thought had to be won over or—a little later and more cynically—run over. But we badly underestimated how quickly others would learn the same lessons we were learning: that there were new opportunities and new responsibilities to directly act politically in ways our personal values demanded. And when those people began to organize and act to defend their cherished and more traditional values about god, religion, family, and authority, and work against what "our" sixties were proclaiming as newer values and a new culture, it was the beginning of another tangible split in America.

Perhaps the cultural split of the sixties was not as severe as the one between early white colonists and Native Americans that ultimately led to genocidal slaughter; or the divisions between the North and South that culminated in over 600,000 Civil War dead. But it was bad enough, and many of the same issues from the sixties feed today's polarization. These days, if you want a quick reminder of the sixties' continuing impact, you can just read the bumper stickers and emblems on people's cars and realize you can easily figure out which side of that long-ago political and cultural split they are on, and what tribe they belong to now.

For the dwindling remnant of leftist sixties survivors, and the well-educated beneficiaries of the new information and services economy in America, it's important to remember our own part in those tribal divisions that helped produce Trump as our current president. While the economic miseries of the non-college educated white working class are a consequence of barely restrained, triumphant global capitalism, the assault on their cultural and social values began in the sixties and has mostly continued since then. Despite having been ignored or trampled on and left behind by an emerging twenty-first century American economy and culture, they formed a noticeable, but usually futile, resistance to that new America. Then their long resistance and anger about a country they had thought of as their own but that seemed to be crowding them out appeared to be rewarded when they reached for the rescue from economic despair that

Trump promised to them. But I think it would be foolish to ignore the role that payback and vengeance played in their voting. The possibility of economic relief *and* a simultaneous opportunity to strike back against despised, sneering, and distant elites—the bankers, businessmen, politicians, academics, and all those people so comfortable with the different culture and country America seemed to be becoming—might have sounded like a pretty good deal.

Of course racism and bigotry were also involved, and Trump and his White House have brought that constellation of ugly, dangerous beliefs and feelings closer to the center of many people's lives and actions. But the rest of us had a bit of a hand in setting the stage for all of that. The initial, partly successful assault on a long-established dominant culture, its demeaning social values, its blatant, accepted racism, and its punitive and isolating sexual and gender expectations, was important, and it remains one of the triumphs of my generation. Even if that fight isn't over, and we now suffer some of the ugly political consequences of helping to split our country into hostile factions and tribes defined by different "values," it was and is a fight that has to be won.

One side in today's political tribal divisions, the "Resistance," more directly and broadly reflects the values, hopes, and commitments that helped define my sixties: a belief in the essential worth of other people, and the belief that personally engaging in political activity is required to meet your obligations to others and to make America a fairer, more just, and better place. The newer movement even echoes some of the internal conflicts and overlapping strategies of those older times, with arguments about the legitimacy, priority, and importance of local issue organizing, electoral politics, peaceful mass protest, and righteous violence.

For example, in an updated version of one of the internal political splits of the late sixties and early seventies about the legitimacy of political violence, nobody today seems willing to claim James Hodgkinson, who shot at Republican congressmen during a baseball practice, as a leading, early member of the Resistance. Nearly everybody labeled him as a loon, and disregarding H. Rap Brown's earlier, perhaps more historically accurate note that violence was as American as apple pie, just about the only people on the left who got any mass media coverage related to Hodgkinson were those who insisted that only nonviolent acts were politically acceptable.

For example, there was Bernie Sanders's statement responding to the fact that Hodgkinson had worked on Bernie's presidential campaign: "Let me be as clear as I can be. Violence of any kind is unacceptable in our society, and I condemn this action in the strongest possible terms. Real change can only come about through nonviolent action, and anything else runs against our most deeply held American values."

When I heard that, I thought most indigenous Americans might have some reasonable arguments and experiences that suggest nonviolence is not quite as deeply embedded in American values as Bernie suggested. Without a deep and abiding faith in the value, importance, and efficacy of violence, there would be a lot more Cherokee tribal members in north Georgia and fewer in places like Oklahoma. Slavery was pretty foundational to the entire American experience. What was that other than violence? And it wasn't calm, reasoned arguments or even boycotts or nonviolent mass demonstrations that interrupted that horror; it was the Civil War.

It also seems self-serving to limit the notion of "political violence" to fists, boots, clubs, knives and guns (and the ever-popular small explosive and incendiary devices) while ignoring the deadly consequences of homelessness and the lack of adequate jobs, health care, and nutritious food that result from the actions—deliberate and otherwise—of corporate and state power. And I'm not even talking about the "point of the spear" violence on the streets by the police.

Corporations (and their political contributions) and governmental authorities and legislatures have managed to avoid having their actions tagged with the disreputable label of "violence." No matter how much their actual and aspirational economic policies reduce taxes on corporations and the very, very rich, while at the same time they reduce the availability of government aid to the elderly poor, it's never talked about as a form of "violence," even when innocent and usually unsuspecting people are hurt by such actions. It's something like the sixties, when many people accepted the continuation of the Vietnam War and a police riot on the streets of Chicago in 1968 as unfortunate things that nevertheless had to be done, while at the same time they denounced the terrible violence of the unarmed and often frightened people who were protesting against the war. Both then and now, there seems to be considerable sophistry in all the high-minded discussion and condemnation of political violence.

In the matter of a different notion that rose to special prominence in the sixties and continues to be important now—a dramatically intensified "identity politics"—I was lucky. I had gotten out of community organizing work in poor neighborhoods in Chicago before I would probably have been quietly, perhaps a little regretfully, but definitely asked to leave or driven out by an emerging and militant black consciousness and its interpretation of the appropriate role whites should play in the struggle against racism in America. So I was able to sidestep what would have been a personal hurt, a hurt Abbie and so many others weren't able to avoid when whites were shut out of the Student Nonviolent Coordinating Committee.

I was luckier still when I was asked by new friends to speak at a gay rights rally in 1969. That gave me an early, easily understood, and accepted introduction to how the empowering language of sixties politics was being broadened and used by new and different groups of people—far beyond the black community and the university students to whom it was first directed.

That language had all along questioned the validity and power of existing authority, and it emphasized resistance to injustice and the cruelty of political and social systems that excluded and isolated its victims. It demanded change. And it shouldn't have come as any surprise that it really was only a matter of time before people began to ask what those fine sounding ideals, intentions, and political goals actually meant in their own lives. How did those ideals translate into how other people see me, how they see and treat us?

Because of course there were groups of people who shared an identity that was fundamental to themselves or who they thought themselves to be—perhaps it was gender, color, race, sexual orientation, national origin, or language. And with that shared part of who they were, they all suffered the same demeaning judgments and penalties that were imposed by external authorities and dominant social systems. And when they talked together, it turned out they had similar dreams for something better in their lives. So they began to organize and act together to achieve those dreams.

There was occasional reluctance to quickly grant complete legitimacy to the claims of oppression and demands for change made by every new group. Sometimes it was an easy decision. The Young Lords—men and women of Puerto Rican descent—had formed early, and by 1970, it was a self-declared left-wing revolutionary nationalist organization that partially mimicked the Panthers in tone and style. Sometimes it was more difficult though. The newly aggressive and unapologetic LGBTQ movement had to struggle for public legitimacy, even from longtime social justice activists. Sometimes it was absolutely unavoidable. The second-wave feminist movement first strengthened the women who helped establish it, then righteously churned through reluctant male leftist public leadership, and then exploded with an open and loud confrontation of the dominant American sexist culture.

The sixties version of identity politics grew to be more personal, intimate, and forceful. It devolved into more separated parts and became less compromising than the earlier expressions and rallying slogans of ethnic and tribal identities in American politics. It too has continued as a relevant part of today's culture and politics, spreading far beyond the boundaries of the Left, and contributes its part to a further splitting between Americans.

There were many other events and shifts in cultural values that marked the sixties and still impact our lives today. Some of them—like the normalization of mass demonstrations—touched my life very directly. But there were others—like the environmental movements and the evolution of the counterculture toward country living and organic farming—that didn't. But there is at least one thing from the sixties that is impossible not to mention, no matter how deliberately selective and minimalist my recounting of those years might be.

Drugs were a prominent part of that time. They were also a big enough part of my own story that they require at least some brief reflection here. I don't suppose many people would list drugs as an unalloyed achievement of the sixties, and it's difficult not to hold the sixties somewhat responsible for increasing the "demand" side of the illicit drug trade. The broader acceptability of recreational drug use was pretty blatant and lasting, and while the softer side of it—weed—may be gaining a wider public tolerance now, not too many people have gotten around yet to thinking that opioids and meth deserve disinterested or resigned acceptance. But I think the lack of opportunity for a reasonable life, one filled with meaningful work that pays a living wage within supportive, viable communities and families, is a bigger cause of the use of that crap than any remnant memories of hippie drug use. However, the hard-core political radicals who, like me, also regularly indulged in recreational drugs and hallucinogenics failed terribly in not explicitly and consistently condemning the use of certain drugs, or discouraging the apolitical, smiling quietude that some of those drugs promised.

But I can't resist suggesting one more, perhaps simple-minded, way of noticing how the sixties are likely still helping shape today's political struggles. I start with the notion that 1968 and 1969 were an exceptionally intense public display of the images and events people are most likely to think about when they think about the sixties. And while I suppose it depended on where you lived and how often you watched television or listened to music or read a newspaper, just about anybody who was between the ages of fifteen and thirty back then was particularly vulnerable to what was happening during those two years.

It's not that younger or older people didn't notice. They might have been participants or fascinated or horrified spectators to a lot of it. But if you were between fifteen and thirty, you really didn't have a lot of choice. You had probably already been noticing some of what was happening earlier in the decade, but 1968 and 1969 were so loud, they created such a cascade of vivid pictures, news, music, war, and people surging on the streets, that the years were almost impossible to ignore. Those events might have been seen as some promise of a better future, or some unending assault on what you thought America was and should be, but it was hard to overlook the fact, to paraphrase both Stephen Stills and Marvin Gaye, that there was something going on. And I think it has been hard for people who were between the ages of fifteen and thirty back then to completely forget those images. I suspect a lot of it helped shape the worldview of those young people as they aged, if only in vague or unconscious ways.

Now take a casual look at the ages of the president, the members of the Supreme Court, and the senior leadership of both parties in the House and Senate. More than 40 percent of them were born between 1938 and 1953, which would put them between the ages of fifteen and thirty in 1968 and 1969. I don't think it's unreasonable to suspect that their experiences of those particular years have had some impact on the tone and direction of the political decisions they are making now. Everyone used to be certain that the political perspectives of the generation that fought in World War II were shaped by their shared experiences of that war. Why would 1968 and 1969 be any different?

And finally, among the noise, accomplishments, and cultural changes of the sixties that are still affecting our political lives, where does the Chicago Eight Conspiracy trial fit in?

It fits in perfectly in two important ways. The trial was the very deliberate and very public use of state power to repress and punish dissent. And of course government authority and power continue to be used today—both in explicit and less obvious ways—to oppress and stifle dissenting voices and the renewed struggle for social and economic justice. At the same time, however, the trial was an equally public but unexpectedly successful display of resistance to state power, and of the capacity and necessity to fight back against threats and oppression. That idea is something the participants in today's political battles understand very well.

While Nixon's Justice Department likely felt satisfied that they had indicted a group of men who they considered to be a representative and symbolic collection of all people and leaders who were threatening established order and values, they badly misjudged some of the consequences of bringing us all together. Because of course, we fought back.

We were not inexperienced, easily intimidated kids, or even adults with an important stake in holding on to some sort of normal life we were leading in an everyday world. John, who was a university instructor, had the closest thing to a "real job" out of any of us. With my part-time research fellowship from Northwestern, I probably ranked a poor second in having any sort of recognizable attachment to the world of work the prosecutors understood. And I had already walked away from all that before the trial even started. Everybody else was floating in a recently emerged, marginal political world, surviving on the generosity of friends and supporters, occasional book contracts, paid magazine articles, speeches on college campuses, or on grandly titled and poorly paid positions at whatever publication or organization could be a temporary home base while they engaged in social change and anti-war politics.

Nothing in our pasts suggested we would be submissive participants in whatever the governments had planned. It was actually quite the contrary. We also weren't isolated individuals. We were instead rooted in a larger community and could draw support from that community to mobilize the substantial resources we needed to effectively respond in the courtroom. More critically, we weren't going to be frightened, and the same skills, political commitments, and determination they had accused us of using to riot, we would use to fight back against them in any way we could.

Worse for the government, their insistence that almost all the bad things that had happened in Chicago were the fault of planned, deliberate manipulations and the acts of eight evil men ran counter to the broad knowledge most people already had of the "crime." After all, the events had been broadcast live into people's homes over several days and nights. And a contrary narrative of the events had already partially formed, where the blame belonged to both demonstrators and the police, and, in some cases, where the police and government shared more of the responsibility for what happened due to their deliberate and illegitimate use of force to punish dissent.

The government's blatant overreach in its exercise of power and threat in the courtroom certainly helped most of the media to pick sides. Even efforts to neutrally describe what was going on largely reinforced our claims about oppression and injustice that we shouted about in the courtroom, in press conferences, and in speeches around the country.

It all added up to an extraordinary prominence for the trial and a new sense of celebrity and notoriety for the defendants. Bobby Seale's courage and dignified contempt of the court, our actions of defiance and openly expressed anger, and our use of satire and laughter to display our utter disrespect for the judge captured the public's attention and imagination. The trial, instead of conveying a more ominous government threat to other people who looked and acted like us, became a rallying cry that resistance was necessary and actually possible, even in what appeared to be the worst circumstances. The ordeal didn't so much frighten young people as it made them angry and more determined than ever to fight back.

And the possibility, the legitimacy of resisting repressive government power in the streets and even in the courts was a notion that stuck in people's heads. In later, rueful private conversations, Lenny Weinglass would sometimes tell me how he would have to patiently explain to new clients why they shouldn't speak out directly in the courtroom as we had, displaying their own brave contempt of government power and repression in their own political trials. Lenny would talk about the differences between our trial—the national media attention, a still growing insurgency in the streets, and an unquestionably biased and hostile judge and court—and the situations his current clients found themselves in.

The government's attempt to use the courts against us, to intimidate and punish, and to define away or trivialize the political purposes and goals of the demonstrations in Chicago in 1968 failed. Instead, the trial and our open confrontations with state power helped strengthen an already existing and growing sixties legacy of resisting injustice and repression.

The government's failure with us, of course, didn't do much to slow down their continued use of the courts to try to stifle and punish political dissent. Recently, the federal government attempted to use the law and the courts in what seemed to me to be a particularly aggressive way against a group of about 200 political demonstrators. In the "J20 Trials," the feds were after people who had protested on the streets of Washington, DC, during Trump's inauguration, and where some demonstrators had deliberately broken windows and caused minor property damage.

Aside from my lingering nostalgia for the rougher edges of street demonstrations, and occasionally wondering whether my political analysis and commitments would mean I would have been part of the "black bloc" of masked anti-fascist resisters if I was younger, the way the feds were throwing around the "conspiracy to riot" charge seemed awfully familiar.

The good news is that, despite the defendants being trapped for months in the same cycle of turmoil, threat, anxiety, paperwork, lawyer meetings, and court appearances that are always the dulling consequences whenever serious criminal charges are used against political work, practically everybody got off. The juries acquitted some defendants and were unable to reach unanimous verdicts on others. The government or the judges dropped many of the initial charges. Nobody was convicted of a felony.

This more recent failure, like the government's earlier failure with us, still won't do much to inhibit their future use of the courts as a weapon against insurgent politics. Worse, it would be foolish, given the current drift of American politics, to count on a continuing, independent judicial system that will reliably set limits on the ruthless efforts by the executive and legislative branches of government to defend existing political and economic power.

But the most important lesson from the sixties and our trial that continues to resonate now is that people can and must resist illegitimate state power and they must help sustain a renewed political struggle for social and economic justice. It is part of how anyone becomes their best self, a responsible citizen and patriot. That was true for me. It is true for anyone.

And while a political life isn't easy, and while frustration, anger, disappointment, fear, and confusion are sometimes pieces of it, I believe there is no more self-respecting, fulfilling life to try to lead. The joys and victories may not come as often as anyone might hope, but when those victories arrive . . . well, I think of the transcendent moments in my life: seeing a near-perfect double rainbow off the rocky, barren Nova Scotia coast, and pulling the car over to just watch in wonder; truly at rest, lying on my back, with my naked sleeping lover's left leg splayed across my own, her head turned to me and cradled in my left arm, her arm and breasts pressed against my body; two vivid orange and black butterflies circling me and then so softly landing on my shoulder and arm; running alongside one of my young daughters, half-holding a bike up, helping her balance, and then suddenly seeing her launch on her bicycle, riding away laughing with unexpected delight.

And when people who are acting politically do have successes, they can then take all of their own transcendent moments, mix them together, add joy with laughter, and share the moment with the closest of friends. That's what even small political victories will feel like. Does that make it all sound a little more enticing? It should. But even better, it's true.

When people are ready to act politically, there is actually quite a bit they can do now. And they can do it pretty easily, without much risk to their reputation or fear of immediate physical harm or potentially devastating future personal consequences. These days, liking a certain group on Facebook, signing an online petition, or making a small monetary donation to a social justice or environmental activist organization is enough to start being political. If you do that, instead of being added to the FBI's list of subversives, the most likely result is that you'll receive a multicolored sticker to put on your car and the opportunity to buy a t-shirt online.

There are also opportunities to engage in politics by participating in public demonstrations, and increasingly, people are being taught and encouraged to actively engage in electoral politics. They're learning how to more effectively influence their local representatives or elect someone new to a state legislative office or Congress. And I agree it's hard to underestimate the political urgency that should push us all toward a stronger focus on local and national electoral politics. Putting in the time and effort to change the makeup of the House and the Senate is justified in the simple hope that it will help slow down bad deeds and harmful laws. This kind of political work also offers a relatively cost-free opportunity for people to actually do things, to act with others and accomplish things that can indisputably be counted as political victories. It might even help point us in the direction of a better world.

But it's important to remember that there are limits to what might be accomplished, even under a more socially liberal and well-intended Congress, and that electoral work doesn't delegitimize or exclude other kinds of political work. The efforts to fight income inequality, racism, corporate interests, abusive police and state power, and denigrating gender norms don't come with a predetermined end date that can tell you whether you've won or lost. That doesn't mean those fights shouldn't be fought. And nobody should be surprised if some of that slower and more prolonged work sometimes includes loud public displays of concern and anger.

However, it's true that nonviolent demonstrations and actions, along with electoral work, provide people a low-cost, nonthreatening way to edge away from being political bystanders or passive victims/citizens. And one aspect of twenty-first century capitalism and anti-democratic, sexist, racist, environmentally destructive ugliness is that they're often easy to act against because those forces are all over the place, very often right in people's neighborhoods. And they're all potential targets for politically inspired actions.

There are ATMs and bank branches, international-brand gas stations, and real estate offices that are branches of national companies or investment firms. There are factories, offices, power plants, and distribution networks that are affiliated with multinational corporations. There are the local offices of the two dominant political parties and elected officials. None of those places have signs in front saying, "Hi! I'm a Local Representative of Globalization, Capitalist Exploitation, and Your Lack of Power Over Your Own Lives." But they could.

The choices of where and how to act will depend partly on what neighbors are already concerned about, what they could be convinced to be concerned about, and what could effectively be shared on social media so that other people might get excited and participate as well. Maybe the issue is about getting more money for the schools or libraries by agitating for a progressive property tax rate that mirrors our progressive income tax rates. Perhaps places like banks—because the economic value of their property is greater—should pay a higher tax rate than the one people pay on their houses. Perhaps towns should pass ordinances requiring national chain grocery stores to place a specific dollar value on the unused food they dispose of, and then make an equivalent cash donation to charitable organizations who distribute food to the hungry.

Doing local work that is explicitly understood as "political" or "morally" required, in a way that is connected to others who are doing the same work, and with little immediate risk of serious personal consequences, is a page right out of the early sixties. When people picketed Woolworth's in northern cities to support the early lunch counter sit-ins down South, there were very few arrests, but a number of people learned that they were the kinds of people who could act on their political beliefs. Because of that, some of them were ready to act at the next opportunity to be "political."

To move progressive politics forward, different kinds of reasonably achievable activities need to be identified and promoted that will initially engage people and then sustain them in what will be a long political struggle. These actions should offer satisfactory ways to express righteous anger, and they should actually accomplish things that can at least occasionally be counted as a victory.

It's important to note here that that I'm mostly talking about activities and acts that are useful. I'm not talking about ideas, values, or the development and dissemination of alternative political visions. A whole lot of people on the left make it a priority to work out better ideas and better stories; they want to be able to provide people with (to borrow a phrase from Naomi Klein) a different outlook and a set of values that can effectively compete against the dominant neoliberal worldview.

It's not that I think inspiring words and stories don't have an important place in political transformations. They do. And I certainly have offered stories here. However, I believe many people have already developed a sense of values and hopes that swirl around notions of social and economic justice. There are already lots and lots of people who want to end racist and sexist oppression. They're willing to listen to how to slow climate change and help people cope with land and oceans that are already hurting. No one needs to hear paragraphs, pages, and chapters from me about sustainable development or capitalist exploitation; they don't need any seductive poetry from me about how life might be and can be better.

I'm not in the visionary business. I still hold on to some sort of Marxist-informed critique about the world, and so I have at least quasi-organized ideas about what must change. I have notions about what life and relationships might be like if there wasn't all the unnecessary suffering and pain from the wounds caused by unrestrained private and corporate wealth and tyrannical, savage state power that is beholden to wealth. But I have to let someone else offer a framework of fundamental values that people might use to critique the everyday world and point them toward the kinds of necessary changes that make sense. I am a little too cynical, a little too damaged to be able to dream sweet dreams with any regularity and then sing those dreams to others.

But it certainly seems that an increasing number of people in America are seeing the ways that abusive government and corporate power prevent the emergence of a freer, more equitable America. And acting together, they are increasingly beginning to fight back and make an enjoyable political mess—if not some kind of revolution—that they hope will lead to something better.

I know "revolution" is a silly kind of word to use these days. It comes burdened with all kinds of unpleasant connotations and ugly historical images that are cultivated by the media and academia. I certainly admit it's mostly a deservedly bad rep. I should stick with talking about "social justice" and making "positive political differences" or "progressive transformations." But I get bored with politically correct and focus-group tested language. I'm old-fashioned, and I actually believe that when serious political changes occur, some people get hurt just as some people get helped.

So talking about "progressive changes," and pretending nothing unpleasant is going to happen to anybody who's on the wrong side of those changes, is self-delusional at best, and just lying to people at worst. If the word "revolution" is occasionally used, it's harder to hide the reality that some people get hurt in politics. However, if required, I'll settle for encouraging people to work for greater social justice that will help make "significant political and economic changes."

As for the actual tactics and strategies to make such changes happen, that's definitely a problem. As Robert Newman points out in *The Fountain at the Center of the World*:

> whenever things came to a head, capitalism could always coopt a movement's reformists and isolate its radicals. Or else it could just start a foreign war. Yes, he could keep telling himself that the billions spent on corporate propaganda and repression were testament to the power people had. It was even true. But still the tyranny prevailed. And all he'd seen in his own life had convinced him that private power was something for which people as yet had no strategy to overthrow.

Well then, we'll just have to work it out as we go along.

I believe the sixties and the Conspiracy Eight Trial are filled with lessons that might help. Then as now, the struggle for social and economic justice had to start with people resisting illegitimate state power by not staying silent and by fighting back against brutality and hate. Some positive social and cultural changes came out of those struggles: laws were created that expanded freedoms and protections for basic rights; and personal values began to change toward a broader acceptance of the differences between people. None of those victories were perfect or complete or perhaps even lasting. And it was hard and often dangerous work.

But the possibility of even partial victories, and the absolute necessity to fight for them, are part of the legacy and lessons of those times. I was fortunate enough to live and work for many years among brave men and women who dedicated themselves to the struggle for social justice. We were all very far from perfect, though we tried to change the world for the better.

I wish I could more effectively hand on to others the commitment to fight injustice and the desire to make the world a more nurturing, safer, and more equitable place for ourselves and our children. I can only hope that that's the direction that peoples' politics take us.

Acknowledgments

A brief acknowledgment of some important people in my story, either not mentioned or not given the attention and words they deserve. I've listed them alphabetically—not in order of appearance or importance—to make it easier for the living to find themselves, and with apologies to those who've changed their names since we knew one another: Stu Albert; Sharon Avery; Richard Ballantine; Bernie Beck; Howie Becker; Bernie Bihari; Judy Gumbo Clavier; Marsha Cohen; Sharon Curtin; Bonnie Dry; Rahm Emanuel; Arthur Epstein; Linda Evans; Justin Finger; Tom and Heather Foley; Abe Foxman; Kinky Friedman; Jim Gordon; Jerry Greenberg; Allen Ginsberg; Anne Gottlieb; Anita Hoffman; Adelle Katz; Eileen Kelly; Marty Kenner; Lillian Kimura; Arthur Kinoy; Sharon Krebs; Paul Kuznekoff; Gary Lefkowitz; Lori Becker Leif; John Lewis; Chuck Longfield; Wolfe Lowenthal; David and Jonathan Lubell; Karen Mann; Bill Moorehead; Phil Ochs; Patty Oldenburg; Ellen Opper; Eric Overman; Robin Palmer; Joe Palombo; Deidre Parham; Abe Peck; John Podesta; Natalie Rosenberg; Chris Rowan; Ed Sanders; Tom Siegel; Morty Stavis; Jerri Suskin; and my children: Alexandra Mann-Weiner; Zoe Mann-Weiner; Noah Weiner; Rachel Weiner; David Weizer; and Rebecca Wilder.

I also want to thank Jeff Kisseloff, whose encouragement and unstinting support made the writing of this book possible, and Anne Trubek, Dan Crissman, and the other good people of Belt Publishing who made it into a real book.

About the Author

Lee Weiner was born and raised on Chicago's South Side. His activist life began with free-speech demonstrations at the University of Illinois in 1960, included community organizing in desperately poor neighborhoods in Chicago, and led to his indictment in the notorious Chicago 7 trial in 1969. His later political work included direct response fundraising for members of Congress and national non-profit organizations. Along the way, he collected a couple of master's degrees and a PhD in sociology. He now lives in Florida.